BECOMING AN AUTHENTIC TEACHER IN HIGHER EDUCATION

The Professional Practices in Adult Education and Human Resource Development Series explores issues and concerns of practitioners who work in the broad range of settings in adult and continuing education and human resource development.

The books are intended to provide information and strategies on how to make practice more effective for professionals and those they serve. They are written from a practical viewpoint and provide a forum for instructors, administrators, policy makers, counselors, trainers, managers, program and organizational developers, instructional designers, and other related professionals.

Editorial correspondence should be sent to

Editor
Professional Practices Series
Krieger Publishing Company
P.O. Box 9542
Melbourne, FL 32902-9542

BECOMING AN
AUTHENTIC
TEACHER
IN HIGHER
EDUCATION

Patricia Cranton

KRIEGER PUBLISHING COMPANY
MALABAR, FLORIDA
2001

Original Edition 2001

Printed and Published by
KRIEGER PUBLISHING COMPANY
KRIEGER DRIVE
MALABAR, FLORIDA 32950

Library of Congress Cataloging-in-Publication Data

Cranton, Patricia.
    Becoming an authentic teacher in higher education / Patricia Cranton.
        p.   cm. — (Professional practices in adult education and human
resource development series)
    Includes bibliographical references and index.
    ISBN 1-57524-119-6 (hardcover : alk. paper)
    1. College teachers—Training of. 2. College teaching. I. Title. II. Series.

    LB1738 .C72 2001
    378.1′2—dc21   00-037118

10   9   8   7   6   5   4   3   2

CONTENTS

PREFACE

A few days after I completed the first draft of *Becoming an Authentic Teacher in Higher Education*, I happened to attend an orientation meeting for new adjunct faculty at the college level. One of the speakers urged the new faculty to never tell students they found the textbook poor, even if they did so. "Tell them it is excellent," she said, "because they trust you as the teacher and will believe the book is excellent if you say it is." Apparently the reason for this deception was to ensure that course evaluations, including the item regarding the textbook, would be high.

Teaching is a specialized form of communication that has as its goal the promotion of learning. Good communication is based on authenticity. If we communicate falsehoods or present ourselves wearing masks, we create an obstacle to meaningful discourse. How can we work toward greater authenticity in our teaching?

I see authenticity as a part of a circle, or perhaps a spiral. We first must understand our Self—our basic nature, preferences, values, and the power of our past experience. We need to separate our sense of Self from the collective of community and society, to know who *we* are, as differentiated from others. This process, called individuation, leads to empowerment. Through understanding our Self, we are able to become free from the constraints of uncritically assimilated values, assumptions, and social norms. We do not run with the herd, we can make choices based on who we are. Authenticity is the expression of one's genuine Self in the community and society. Empowerment leads us to authenticity. The circle closes, or the spiral moves upward, when authentic expression leads us to further differentiate ourselves from others.

Becoming an Authentic Teacher in Higher Education is written primarily for teachers in higher education, but will be equally meaningful for teachers in all adult education contexts. Faculty developers in colleges and universities will also find the book to be of interest in their work. Graduate students looking forward to a teaching career in the academic world and novice faculty members will find the personal and realistic approach to understanding teaching appealing and refreshing. The purpose of this book is to illustrate in a practical, clear, and concrete fashion how we can work toward becoming more authentic in our teaching. Using examples, case studies, stories, and exercises, it leads teachers through the various facets of authenticity, including understanding one's Self, seeing how Self and Teacher can be integrated, relating to students, working in a social context, and continuing to grow and develop.

In the literature on teaching in higher education, lengthy lists of the characteristics of good teaching are identified. The implication of such lists is that good teachers master as many of these skills and integrate into their behavior as many of these characteristics as possible. I believe that there are many different and often contradictory ways of being a good teacher. Becoming a good teacher involves understanding oneself and from that understanding, building a personal ideal of practice. In other words, becoming a good teacher means becoming an authentic teacher, true to one's Self.

Becoming an Authentic Teacher in Higher Education begins with two chapters dedicated to understanding our Self. In Chapter 1, I explore our understanding of our basic sense of Self and our psychological preferences. In Chapter 2, I turn to the powerful influence of past experiences on our perception of our Self and the significance of our cherished, but often unarticulated, values. Both chapters include exercises designed to foster self-awareness.

In Chapter 3, I inquire into the social construct of *the good teacher* and urge readers to identify their own personal teaching strengths within that construct. This theme is carried on into Chapter 4 where I suggest we examine our own stories as teachers and contemplate how we might integrate our Self into our teaching roles. Listening to others' stories can help us understand our own story. Chapter 5 contains stories from four authentic teachers.

Being an authentic teacher means being able to communicate with students while remaining true to one's Self. In Chapter 6, I describe different kinds of relationships we have with students and provide exercises to help in identifying them and making them more meaningful. Chapter 7 moves the discussion of authenticity out of the context of the classroom and student relationships into the larger contexts of our discipline, institution, community, state, and society.

Individuation, growth, and development foster authenticity. In Chapter 8, I discuss personal and professional development, focusing on how each contributes to the other as we integrate Self and Teacher.

ACKNOWLEDGMENTS

I would like to thank those people with whom I engaged in good and meaningful conversations on the nature of authentic teaching: Janice Clark, Kirsten Graham, Peter Lane, and Susan Wilcox. I would especially like to thank Laurence Robert Cohen who generously gave of his time to critique the manuscript. His many insightful and thoughtful comments contributed greatly to the final product.

THE AUTHOR

Patricia Cranton received her B.Ed. degree (1971) and M.Sc. degree (1973) from the University of Calgary and her Ph.D. degree (1976) from the University of Toronto.

Patricia's primary research interests have been self-directed and transformative learning, teaching and learning in higher education, and faculty development. She was selected as an Ontario Distinguished Scholar in 1991 in recognition of her research and writing on teaching and learning in higher education. She received the Ontario Confederation of University Faculty Association's Teaching Award in 1993 and the Lieutenant Governor's Laurel Award in 1994 for an outstanding contribution to university teaching.

In addition to her numerous articles and conference presentations, Patricia Cranton's books include *Planning Instruction for Adult Learners* (1989), *Working with Adult Learners* (1992), *Understanding and Promoting Transformative Learning* (1994), *Professional Development as Transformative Learning* (1996), *No One Way: Teaching and Learning in Higher Education* (1998), and *Personal Empowerment through Type* (1998).

From 1976 to 1986, Patricia Cranton was at McGill University in the Centre for Teaching and Learning and the Department of Educational Psychology and Counselling. From 1986 to 1996, she was at Brock University in the Faculty of Education. She founded Brock University's Instructional Development Office and directed it from 1991 to 1996. She is now professor of adult education at the University of New Brunswick.

CHAPTER 1

Understanding Your Self

How often, in our teaching, do we try to be someone other than who we are? The quiet teacher berates herself for not being a dynamic lecturer. The creative teacher complains that he is not well organized. The organized teacher knows she is not flexible enough. The caring teacher feels he neglects to keep up to date in his discipline. The practical teacher sees herself as not being innovative enough.

I believe there are many different and often contradictory ways of being a good teacher. The creative, intuitive teacher may be stifled if we give him a structured set of instructional design principles to follow, complete with objectives and sequencing procedures. The teacher who cares deeply and personally for her students may find herself paralyzed if we insist she incorporate new technologies into her classroom. The social construct of the *Good Teacher* parallels that of the *Good Mother.* Expectations are high.

Our development as teachers consists of a process of self-awareness and acceptance, coming to see that we cannot be all the things the *Good Teacher* is expected to be, and understanding that who we are as human beings is at the core of becoming an authentic teacher. From there, we can learn how to relate to students as one person relating to another. We can see our Self as a member of a learning group. We can see our Self as a teacher working within a context. Then, our personal and professional growth become two strands of the same process—the maturing, developing adult and the transforming teacher.

In this chapter, I focus on understanding our Self. This provides the foundation for separating out the strands of who we are and who we think we should be, based on others' perceptions of good teaching. First, I ask, Who are you, really? How do you define your Self? Second, I question the preferences we have in life. What is our true basic nature? How do we prefer to be? How often are we doing things that are not congruent with our natural preferences? When do we feel like imposters sitting at the "teacher's desk"?

These questions do not comprise the totality of an individual. In Chapter 2, I go on to consider the role our experiences and values play in forming our Self. Also, I am deliberately leaving out such major components of the Self as knowledge, expertise, intelligence, and creativity. This is not because I do not believe they are important aspects of shaping ourselves as teacher. In fact, many of them will come up as we go on. In the beginning, what I want to do is to encourage a delving into the center of the Self, the soul perhaps, as John Dirkx (1997) would say. For it is there, I think, that we can conceptualize ourselves as authentic teachers.

WHO ARE YOU, REALLY?

I adapted this heading from the title of Daryl Sharp's (1995) book, *Who Am I Really?*, an exploration of personality and soul. Sharp asks: What is personality? What differentiates an individual from a member of the collective? Where does vocation fit in? and What is the role of education? In an earlier book, Sharp (1987, p. 94) suggests that "with any attempt to understand oneself, there is no substitute for prolonged reflection." Perhaps. But perhaps prolonged reflection is not natural to all individuals. Daryl Sharp may well be a reflective person himself; Carl Jung, upon whom Sharp bases his work, was definitely a reflective person. However, we must be careful not to generalize from ourselves to others, or from others to ourselves. As teachers, we cannot expect our students to be like us, nor can we expect our teaching self to be like the models held up to us. I try, in asking "Who are you, really?" to ask the question from enough angles and perspectives that the personalities of many different types of teachers will be engaged.

A colleague came as a guest to one of my graduate adult education classes and had us do a small exercise which has stayed in my mind. Without elaboration, he asked us to list ten nouns or phrases we would use to describe our identity, our Self. We could write, for example, mother, teacher, writer, squash player, wife. He then asked us to cross off two from the list that were less essential to our identity. We then had to cross off two more, and two more, until finally he asked us to cross off the last remaining descriptors. I do not think I was the only person in the group who refused to cross items off near the end of the activity. When he insisted, I discretely turned my paper over, but left the words on the list. The exercise was debriefed in relation to the topic of the session, but its impact was dramatic in another way. After class, several people were quietly asking each other, "Did you really cross everything off?"

The words we use to describe ourselves are powerful indicators of how we see ourselves. They tell the story of who we are in relation to others, what our work is, what we value, and sometimes how we function in the world or see the world. In Exercise 1.1, I pose this basic question and suggest various ways of working with it, each of which might be suitable to people of different natures.

The first part of understanding ourselves is to see how we define our basic Self. What constructs or perspectives do we hold about ourselves? What words might we list in this exercise that if they were suddenly not true, we would lose our sense of Self? I might be, for example, a squash player, but not lose my sense of Self if I move to a remote area where no squash courts are available. On the other hand, if I define myself as a teacher and I can no longer teach, I may lose all sense of who I am. Another person, for whom playing squash is a deep part of his Self, might suffer great trauma if he were injured and could no longer play. But, perhaps this same person could give up teaching without a second thought. I see the first part of this exercise as being equivalent to content reflection (Mezirow, 1991). We are asking what we are, who we are, what our construct of our Self is.

Exercise 1.1. Who Are You, Really?

Part One. *Ten nouns or noun phrases that define my Self:*

1. _____ 2. _____

3. _____ 4. _____

5. _____ 6. _____

7. _____ 8. _____

9. _____ 10. _____

Part Two. *How did I come to see myself this way?*

Do I define myself this way through experience?
Do I define myself this way through a vision of how I want to be?
Do I logically and autonomously choose to define myself this way?
Do I define myself this way in relation to others or others' values?

Part Three. *Why does each descriptor matter at all?*

Does it matter because it is what I currently do?
Does it matter because it relates to vision of how I want to be?
Does it matter because it is my own independent and reasonable choice?
Does it matter because it is related to people I care for or to social expectations?

The second part of getting at our essential Self is to consider how it came to be that we saw ourselves this way. Mezirow (1991) describes process reflection, trying to understand how we came to hold an assumption or have a certain perspective. However, it may not be through reflection that every person can come to this understanding. In a recent presentation, I asked people to work in groups formed on the basis of their psychological type preferences (Cranton, 1998a). When they discussed the core process involved in changing their basic assumptions, the various groups described their minds as working in quite different ways. In Part Two of the activity suggested in Exercise 1.1, I have listed four different kinds of questions that might help us to understand how we came to hold a certain view of ourselves. It may be that all or most of our descriptors have come to be through the same process, or it may be that different aspects of ourselves have developed along separate routes. For example, I might see myself as a teacher simply because I teach, it is my current and past experience, it is what I do. Or, I might have come to see myself as a writer through a lifelong dream or a vision of what I want to be. Another person might have come to see himself as a teacher because it was a part of his family life and the expectation of those he cared for. Perhaps his mother and father were both teachers, he grew up in that mileu, he valued what his family valued, and he came to see himself as a teacher. Still another person could have made an independent and autonomous choice: "no matter what anyone says, I know I want to be a teacher."

Mezirow (1991) suggests that when we question the very premise of something—why is this important in the first place? who cares about this?—we are most likely to open ourselves up to another way of seeing things. Maybe it's not important. Maybe it could be another way. In the third part of understanding our Self (Exercise 1.1), I suggest that we also ask those kinds of questions of how we see ourselves. Why is this important? Should I keep this as a way of seeing myself? Although I may have come to see myself as a teacher simply because I teach, it may now be important for me to maintain that perspective because I care deeply about my students, present and future. Another person may have defined himself as a teacher through having a vision of the role of teaching in society but may now, after many disillusioning years of practice, maintain his perspective of himself as a teacher because it is a social expectation or obligation from which he feels he cannot escape.

In questioning the premises of our self-definitions, it may also be helpful to ask, What would happen if I did *not* describe myself that way? What if I were forced to change that way of seeing myself? Would I still be my Self if I were not a teacher? Not a father? Not a squash player? Not a pianist? Are there other, more central, descriptors that I have not listed?

Many of us do not spend a lot of time questioning who we are or how we see ourselves. We run from home and family responsibilities to the classroom, then to meetings with students, committee meetings, another class, back to the office to read and comment on some student work, write some memos, answer the phone, check e-mail, and finally out again to pick up children or run errands, take care of things at home, and prepare again for the next day, or perhaps try to work a little on a paper we hope to publish. Considering how we define ourselves, the sources of those perceptions, and why they are important may be only fleeting thoughts or images, or these questions may not trouble us at all. Yet, I argue that if we do not know who we are as human beings, it is very difficult to know who we are as teachers. Without a sound self-knowledge, we will find ourselves trying to be all the things that the *Good Teacher* is supposed to be, many of which go against our basic nature.

PREFERENCES

Given the many preferences individuals have, including everything from teaching and learning style to a predilection for certain types of music or food, it initially seems foolish to try to examine personal preferences in this context. However, I believe that our preferences for psychological attitudes and functions (Jung, [1921] 1971) underlie a great number of our more specific inclinations. Here, I outline the general framework of psychological type theory before turning to an examination of personal preferences.

Jung defines two attitudes and four psychological functions which work together to create eight patterns of personality or "types" of people. Our attitudes toward the world may be more introverted or more extraverted. When we have an introverted attitude, we are focused on the inner Self and tend to want to exclude or ignore things in the outside world. When the introverted person perceives or judges things from the external (to the Self) environment, she personalizes the process in order to make it her own. She concentrates on how she feels or thinks about what she observes or experiences.

On the other hand, when we have an extraverted attitude, we focus on the external or objective world. We are interested in things around us and take them for what they are, without personalizing them. No person is entirely introverted or extraverted, but most of us have a preference for one attitude or the other. We may adopt one attitude in one context, such as in our professional life, and another in another context, such as in our home life. Even so, at the core of our Self, either introversion or extraversion is likely to be more natural and comfortable.

Two different psychological functions can be used to perceive things. Using sensing, we take in things around us through our five senses. Using intuition, we form perceptions that come seemingly out of nowhere in the form of images, visions, or sweeping pictures. A person who is more introverted personalizes his perceptions.

Similarly, two different psychological functions can be used to make judgments. If we use thinking, we form judgments in a logical analytical fashion. Feeling, on the other hand, is a function that operates based on values. People use the feeling function to quickly evaluate the things they perceive, and in doing so to maintain harmony between their Self and others. Again, a person who is more introverted personalizes the thinking or the feeling process.

According to the theory, each person has a dominant or strongly preferred function, one of the four—sensing, intuition, thinking, or feeling. That function is either introverted or extraverted—turned inward or focused on the external world. Each person also has a less strong secondary or auxiliary function. If their dominant function is perceiving, then they have a secondary function for judging, and vice versa. That function, too, can be either introverted or extraverted and need not be in the same attitude as the dominant function. A person could have a dominant extraverted thinking function and a secondary preference for introverted intuition, for example.

Some people do not have clearly defined psychological preferences. According to Jung, they are undifferentiated from the collective of humanity. Or, in other words, they have not fully or successfully separated from their family or community in order to define their unique Self. The clarification and understanding of our psychological type preferences is a developmental process that may occur early or later in life. Jung sees it as a lifelong developmental process.

In Exercise 1.2, I present a checklist that can be used to help determine psychological type preferences. This checklist is intended to be a self-awareness exercise and is not an established psychological inventory (for a full instrument, see Cranton & Knoop, 1994, 1995). By selecting the words we see as describing ourselves, we can quickly see which functions we prefer to use. It may be useful to draw a profile of these preferences, such as is shown in Figure 1.1. In this example, the individual shows a strong preference for the thinking function, especially on the extraverted side. Her secondary preference is for the sensing function, again on the extraverted side. Viewing our psychological type preferences as a profile rather than as a label or category maintains the complexity of the Self. No person uses just one function, but we can usually see patterns in the way we choose to be.

In the self-awareness exercise I present for understanding the Self (Exercise 1.1), I suggest guiding questions for examining how we came to see ourselves that way and why the perception is important to us. These questions are parallel to Mezirow's (1991) process and premise reflection. The four questions in the exercise are designed to represent the four functions of sensing, intuition, thinking, and feeling. It is my belief that the process by which we come to understand ourselves is, in itself, grounded in our psychological type preferences. I ask people to consider whether their sense of self is based on experience (developed through the sensing function), vision (intuitive function), logical choice (thinking function), or others' values (feeling function).

Several years ago in a course I was teaching, students were engaged in a critical reflection exercise. Peter, who had a clear preference for extraverted sensing, was hurt and bewildered to find that critical reflection did not come easily to him. "I learn," he said, "I change, I develop, but not through *reflection*!" Peter's objection to the exercise and hence to the theory not only stayed in my mind but colored my entire perspective on how individuals grow and develop. It is for this reason that, here, I attempt to balance the kinds of self-awareness questions among the psychological type preferences.

Can we question our psychological preferences in the same way? Content reflection, the first level, yields a description of our preferences, such as the one that can be obtained in Exercise 1.2. The second level, considering how we came to be the way we are, may be more difficult. Jung ([1921] 1971) considers our preferred functions to be either innate or in place at a very early age. We may or may not accept this, but it does seem that individual's profiles are amazingly stable over time and across situations. On the other hand, we also know that people who have an undifferentiated or unclear profile have not yet developed their preferences, and they may do so as a part of conscious growth. Also, many materials based on psychological type theory include guidelines and suggestions for the development of attitudes and functions. It seems that we cannot rule out type development as a process; therefore, it is reasonable for us to review the process by which we may have come to have our preferences.

In Exercise 1.3, I propose the same kind of activity as we used to understand our perception of the Self. Part Two contains questions related to how our preferences may have developed or emerged. Since the questions themselves are designed to reflect type preferences, it is likely that only one or two of them will seem to be relevant. For example, a participant in a workshop on teaching and learning, Colleen, listed extraverted feeling as her first preference and extraverted sensing as her second pref-

Exercise 1.2. Psychological Type Preferences

Put an X next to each word that describes you.

____active   ____practical   ____down-to-earth
____realistic   ____experiential   ____factual
____sensible   ____nonreflective   ____fashionable
____sensuous

(How many X's? Extraverted Sensing= _____*)*

____enterprising   ____imaginative   ____easily bored
____unrealistic   ____inventive   ____resourceful
____original   ____future-oriented   ____creative
____visionary

(How many X's? Extraverted Intuition= _____*)*

____analytical   ____decisive   ____organized
____critical   ____resistant   ____principled
____consistent   ____fair   ____idealistic
____autocratic

(How many X's? Extraverted Thinking= _____*)*

____accepting   ____harmonious   ____responsive
____agreeable   ____sympathetic   ____adaptable
____sociable   ____uncritical   ____susceptible
____compassionate

(How many X's? Extraverted Feeling= _____*)*

____discerning   ____painstaking   ____impressionable
____careful   ____meticulous   ____vulnerable
____observant   ____modest   ____precise
____conscientious

(How many X's? Introverted Sensing= _____*)*

____clairvoyant   ____prophetic   ____psychic
____imaginative   ____mystical   ____eccentric
____enigmatic   ____mysterious   ____quixotic
____indifferent

(How many X's? Introverted Intuition= _____*)*

____analytical   ____decisive   ____reflective
____argumentative ____thoughtful   ____unyielding
____consistent   ____logical   ____questioning
____contemplative

     (How many X's? Introverted Thinking= _____*)*

____amiable   ____enigmatic   ____receptive
____compassionate ____gentle   ____elusive
____considerate   ____intense   ____placating
____complex

     (How many X's? Introverted Feeling= _____*)*

---

erence. In Part Two of the exercise she felt that her preferences had been strongly influenced by her relationships with other people, especially her family and close friends. "I don't like to be out of synch with others," she said, "so I adapt to the people I care for, I work hard to understand them and be one with them. This genuinely becomes my own preference; it's not "put on" like you might think." Colleen could not identify with the other questions in Part Two. She simply said, "no" in response to each of them.

In Part Three, we can question the premise that psychological type theory is helpful in explaining our Self. Again, the four kinds of questions reflect the four psychological functions. Here, however, a person who has become convinced of the value or validity of type theory may answer all of the questions in a positive manner. When we have accepted the premise underlying an approach, the style of questioning is not relevant. To challenge that premise, we would also want to seriously consider questions from every perspective.

When I asked Colleen, who had a newly acquired appreciation of psychological type theory, to consider the questions in Part Three of the exercise, she answered each with an enthusiastic "yes." A more skeptical workshop or course participant would raise each of these questions and more (for example, see Brailey, 1998). It is the skeptic's response that accurately represents premise reflection as Mezirow (1991) describes it.

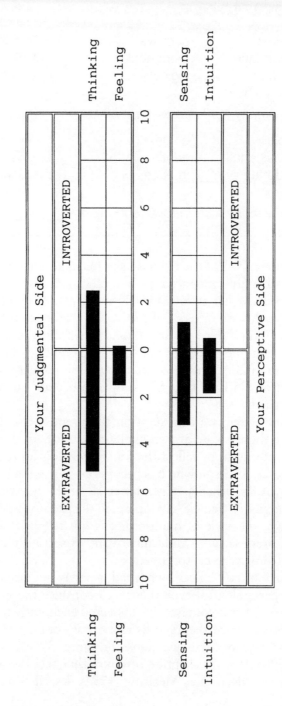

Figure 1.1 Psychological Type Profile

Exercise 1.3. Exploring Psychological Preferences

Part One: What are my preferences?

Using results from the checklist in Exercise 1.2 or a profile such as Figure 1.1, list your strongest perceptive and your strongest judgmental function:

1. _____   2. _____

Part Two: How did I come to have these preferences?

Have my preferences developed through what I have done in life, through my experiences?
Are my preferences based on an image or vision of how I want to be?
Did I consciously and deliberately choose to be the way I am?
Have I developed my preferences through interactions with others, including family, friends, and the society I live in?

Part Three: Why are psychological preferences relevant at all?

Does psychological type make sense in relation to the reality of what I do and have done?
Does psychological type theory provide a new opportunity for looking into my Self or a way to form a new self-image?
Is psychological type a logical and coherent way of seeing myself?
Does psychological type explain the way people get along with each other and adapt to their social world?

SUMMARY

As teachers, our primary role is interaction with others. We work with students and often with colleagues or administrators to promote student learning and development. In order to interact well with others, we need to be genuinely ourselves. A person playing a role or behaving in ways that are contradictory to her natural way of being cannot maintain the kind of authentic connection with students that leads to meaningful learning. It is the presence of the teacher as a person that distinguishes classroom or group learning from learning via technology, reading, or independent study. I think we would all agree that the presence of a teacher is central in our educational endeavors. No one is willing to argue that distance education or computer-managed learning experiences, despite their advantages, can entirely replace working with a living teacher.

The teacher needs to know herself as a person in order to know herself as a teacher. She needs to know herself as a person so as to have good and satisfying relationships with others in her teaching role. In this chapter, I worked through two aspects of coming to understand one's Self: a basic definition of how we see ourselves followed by a consideration of psychological type preferences. For each of these areas, I proposed content, process, and premise questions for deepening our understanding. I suggested these questions from the perspective of four different psychological functions.

CHAPTER 2

Understanding Experiences and Values

The way we see the world and what we come to value is determined in large part by what we have experienced. Jerry Apps, in *Teaching from the Heart* (1996), skillfully weaves his experiences in rural Wisconsin into his perspective on teaching. Another person may be shaped by educational experiences, and someone else by relationships with others. People continually make meaning out of experiences, revise perspectives, and adopt new points of view based on new experiences. This process forms who we are and what we value.

According to transformative learning theory (Cranton, 1994; Mezirow, 1991), the way we make meaning out of experiences determines our *habitual expectations* or our *habits of mind*—our assumptions, beliefs, values, and perspectives. If I have only experienced classes in which someone tells me what to learn, I will expect that to occur the next time I attend a class. It is likely that I will value a good, clear, directive teacher, because this is what I have experienced. Encountering a different type of experience may lead me to question the value I hold about teaching, and even revise my perspective, but it may not. In adulthood, our values are strong, not easily open to revision.

In this chapter, I first suggest considering the significant experiences that have formed our sense of Self, questioning each as to how it came to be significant, and asking why the experience matters. As in Chapter 1, I encourage the asking of content, process, and premise reflection questions. I then work through an exercise to help us articulate the values we hold and question their source and importance. Increasing our self-awareness in relation to these dimensions helps us to see who we are as people. Becoming an authentic teacher depends on understanding our Self.

EXPERIENCE

We cannot separate our sense of Self from our experiences. All human beings have a need to understand and order the meaning of their experiences, to integrate new experiences with old, and avoid the threat of chaos or the feeling of meaninglessness. If we saw a green sky upon awakening tomorrow morning, we would not just say, "oh look, the sky is green" and go on about our daily business. We would seek to understand why we were seeing a green sky. Our Self shapes our experiences and our experiences shape our Self. I am who I am because of where and how I grew up; I have been formed through my relationships with others, where I have traveled, what I have learned as a student, and what I have learned and experienced as a teacher. At the same time, who I am, my basic nature, has influenced how I have interpreted my experiences. Two people going through the same event may interpret it in very different ways and this is, at least in part, related to our psychological preferences and the experiences we have had prior to this one.

An important component of understanding ourselves, and consequently understanding who we are as teachers is to explore, reflect on, and review the significant experiences of our lives. These experiences may be related primarily to teaching, or, depending on the individual, it may be equally important to reflect on experiences outside of our professional lives. These experiences or events may have formed us, validated us, or changed our perspectives. Brookfield (1995), in his book, *Becoming a Critically Reflective Teacher*, recommends using critical incidents as a method of encouraging reflection. He suggests exercises in which we think of the best or worst experience we have had, usually related to teaching or learning, within the last six months or year. He advises that we work through a series of questions designed to bring out and challenge our underlying assumptions—when we see an incident as critical, some of our fundamental beliefs or values will be revealed in the incident. I suggest that for our purposes here we do not consider a specific time frame, but rather recall significant experiences from any period in our lifetime—those that stand out in memory as having changed our way of being. These experiences may, but need not, relate to teaching.

In Exercise 2.1, I provide a variety of ways of contemplating the experiences that have shaped us. First, we need to recall what such experiences may have been. This should be done without judgment or review; it should be those incidents that first come to mind when we think about things that have significantly altered our lives. Ten is an arbitrary number. It is quite possible that only three or four events are momentous enough to include. As in the exercises in Chapter 1, the first part of the process is what Mezirow (1991) would call content reflection. We ask ourselves, simply, "What happened?"

As an example, I might have made the following list in response to Part One of the exercise.

1. *Going to graduate school*

2. *Becoming a mother*

3. *Break-up of my marriage*

4. *Getting my first faculty position*

5. *Taking a course in European literature*

6. *Going into adult education*

7. *Getting my first book published*

8. *Moving to Tennessee*

9. *Working with a certain graduate student*

10. *My mother's death*

I did not list these events in any kind of order, chronological or otherwise; I listed them as they came to mind when I reflected

---

Exercise 2.1. Contemplating Signficant Experiences

Part One. Up to ten experiences that have significantly changed my Self:

1. _____   2. _____

3. _____   4. _____

5. _____   6. _____

7. _____   8. _____

9. _____   10. _____

Part Two. How did I come to see each experience as significant?

Is it significant simply because it happened?
Is it significant because it fulfilled a vision?
Is it significant because I deliberately and autonomously made it happen?
Is it significant because it brought me into harmony with others values?

Part Three. Why do I care about these experiences at all?

Does it matter because it is a part of my personal history?
Does it matter because it continues to form my future?
Does it matter because I chose to make it important?
Does it matter because it is important to people I care about?

---

on the question. If I were to review the list, I might decide to delete some items or add others, but it is probably most meaningful to work with the original list.

In Part Two of the activity, we go back and ask ourselves how each of these experiences came to be pivotal in our lives. This need not be a logical or rational process by any means, and we should not ask how we decided to list them, but instead, how they came to be significant. I include guiding questions, intended to be meaningful to people of different personality preferences.

As an example, I take the first item from my sample list: going to graduate school. How did I come to see that experience as profound? Was it simply because it happened? No, it did not simply happen. It was a difficult and conscious decision. Did it fulfil a vision? Partly, but not a clear vision. The vision was internal, more a way of seeing myself than an articulated intuition. The third question seems to be the most relevant. It was a significant experience because it was a deliberate, independent, and logical decision to change the course of my life.

Another person's investigation of the same incident could be quite different. A decision to continue with higher education may be significant for practical or financial reasons, because it was a social expectation, or because a person was following in the footsteps of a mentor. Individuals may not have "reasons" at all, but intuitions, feelings, or practicalities that lead them to include various items as significant experiences. The process by which we come to consider an incident important and meaningful varies from person to person. Understanding this process helps us to know our Self.

Challenging the premise of why we find a specific experience significant is not easy to do. We have listed it; we have identified how we came to see it as significant; now we need to ask why it is an item on the list in the first place. Examining premises encourages us to question the underlying assumptions upon which we base many life decisions. For example, if I reexamine "going to graduate school" as an item on my significant experiences list, I would ask myself "Why is this on the list in the first place? Why do I consider this important enough to include? Who cares about going to graduate school?" The first thought may be, "Naturally, it's on the list, it determined the whole direction of my career and life." Yes, that is why it was included originally. But, what else underlies it? In Part Three of Exercise 2.1, I list some questions that might be useful. For some people, discussion of such questions with a trusted colleague or friend is helpful. As Brookfield (1995) so aptly wrote, it is difficult to see the back of one's head in the mirror. If we hold up another mirror, engage the help of another person, we can often see much more clearly.

The four questions address different ways in which individuals may determine significance. Of course, there are more than four possible questions, but these may serve to start the process. For some individuals, the fact that an experience was simply an important part of their personal history is what makes it significant. No other motives lurk beneath the surface. For others, the premise of significance is based on the future rather than the past—the event continues to form the future. What makes an incident critical can be based on intellectual considerations, on a logical, analytical process. Or, it can be critical in light of how it changed or formed relationships with others.

When I examine the premise of my including "going to graduate school" in my list, I find that it was significant because I acted contrary to the social norms of my community and family. I acted against all odds—it was not financially nor practically feasible for me to make this decision; it was not what anyone expected or wanted me to do. The premise underlying my finding this significant is that it is "good" to be independent and to work toward a personal goal in spite of all obstacles.

Contemplating questions about our experiences is just one way of coming to understand them. Brookfield (1995) advocates the use of autobiographies from which we can sometimes gain extremely interesting insights. Keeping a journal and especially reviewing old journals for those individuals who are regular journal writers, setting up a discussion group with colleagues, looking through old photograph albums, or interviewing family members or others who have known us for an extended period of time can all act as sparks for discerning the magnitude of past experiences in shaping our current Self.

VALUES

The things we value, attach importance to, or cherish are usually unquestioned or sometimes even unarticulated. We take

them for granted, and often they have been uncritically assimilated. That is, they have been absorbed, without thought or reflection, from our family background, community, culture, or
professional life. Some of our values are a part of our basic nature or the product of our psychological preferences. Heimlich
and Norland (1994) suggest that values are complex, resistant
to change, and have an influence on both our behavior and other
aspects of our Self. We may not even be aware of when and how
our values are influencing the way we act. Because of this, it can
be quite difficult to name our values.

We have frames of reference and habits of mind (Mezirow,
2000) acting as filters for interpreting experiences. If both you
and I hear someone telling an obvious untruth, I may react with
dismay, anger, or hurt because telling an untruth contradicts my
values, the way I think people should behave. You, on the other
hand, may understand the reasons for the lie or not be bothered
by it, and react very differently. Our values filter the way we
interpret the same event.

Values exist in several domains, including:

- sociolinguistic, related to our social norms, culture, and customs
- moral or ethical
- philosophical or religious
- psychological, including self-concept, parental prohibitions,
  and personality traits
- aesthetic, including standards and judgments (Mezirow, 2000).

People who work to help others name their values usually
employ values clarification exercises of various kinds. These activities typically include a description of a dilemma or situation
in which values-based decisions need to be made. The scenario
might present a number of people in a life-threatening predica-
ment such as a sinking boat. Participants may need to decide
who of a limited number of people should go on a life raft—
young mother, teacher, carpenter, wise old man, and so forth.
In making the decisions, participants' values are expressed. Less
dramatic variations of the exercise include deciding which tools

or materials to take along, or they do not include a forced-choice element.

Given that values are hard to bring to the surface, how can we explore this aspect of our Self? Our values are clearly critical in understanding ourselves as teachers. Heimlich and Norland (1994) provide a *Teaching Values Scale* that helps us to see whether we value content, environment, teacher, group, or student in our practice, but I suggest that we first need to examine the deeper, more personal values that underlie our professional values.

In Table 2.1, I provide examples of values that may help us to start identifying the values we hold. The list is not intended to be comprehensive, but it should at least give a point of departure for listing other values. It may be helpful to go through these examples and ask whether or not these are values we hold. Then, once we are on our way, more appropriate words or phrases are likely to come to mind.

In Exercise 2.2, I suggest a similar set of questions to those I gave for contemplating significant experiences and for defining the Self. In Part One, I recommend listing 10, or less, values we hold deeply or cherish. These should not be superficial, but genuine convictions.

When I asked a colleague to respond to this exercise, he listed:

1. *Independence*

2. *Quietude*

3. *Peace of mind*

4. *Financial security*

He felt that he could not list more than four *cherished* values.

In Part Two of the exercise, the guiding questions relate to how we came to hold each value. Once identified, it may be easier to recognize the source of values, but it could also be helpful to discuss this process with another person. When I asked these questions of the colleague who listed his values, his answers were brief and definite. We took his first value, independence.

Table 2.1   Examples of Values

Personal Values:

Knowledge	Independence	Love
Meaning	Trust	Openness
Courage	Integrity	Comfort
Adventure	Inner peace	Equality
Happiness	Pleasure	Relationships
Self-esteem	Compassion	Religion
Honesty	Beauty	Possessions
Self-actualization	Development	Empowerment

Professional Values:

Security	Autonomy	Effectivness
Job satisfaction	Achievement	Money
Being with others	Success	Recognition
Expertise	Responsibility	Cooperation
Stability	Competence	Power
Quality	Hard work	Loyalty
Efficiency	Authority	Being liked
Social change	Growth	Learning

He indicated that it was based on bad experience—there were times in his life when he was not independent and thereby came to develop this value. When I asked if the value was a vision of how things should be, he responded "yes," but then said he did not deliberately choose to value independence, it simply was the way he saw himself. He was equally clear that he did not come to hold this value because others did.

In Part Three of the exercise, I recommend questioning the premise underlying each value. Why is this value important? Can I conceive of my life without this value? What would the world look like if everyone held this value? If no one held it? Our goal is not to challenge or change what we believe, but to understand its importance in our lives. In Exercise 2.2, I give four questions that can be applied to each listed value.

When my colleague applied these questions to his value of independence, he was again very sure of his responses. He did not value independence because he always valued it; quite the opposite, in fact. He did see it as a part of his vision of the world,

---

Exercise 2.2. Identifying Values

Part One.   List up to ten cherished values:

1. _____   2. _____

3. _____   4. _____

5. _____   6. _____

7. _____   8. _____

9. _____   10. _____

Part Two.   How did I come to have each value?

Do I value this based on experience?
Do I value this as a part of a vision of how things should be?
Did I deliberately and autonomously choose this value?
Do I value what others value?

Part Three.   Why is each value important to me?

Do I value this because I have always valued it?
Is this value a part of my vision of the world or the future?
Is this value important because I have thought it through logically?
Is this value important because it is a part of my social world?

---

and here he underlined "my" to emphasize that this was a personal view. He did not expect others to share his vision. He did not find his value to be significant because it was thought through, nor did he see it as a part of his social world. The premise underlying his value was that he could envision how he wanted things to be, and his visions formed his values.

For another person, values may well be based on rational thought, or on expectations of others and social norms. Some individuals base their values on experience. What has happened to them guides the way they see the world. They make meaning out of their experience and when this is positive and rewarding, it is repeated and values form.

Many people, in reviewing the guiding questions in Exercise 2.2, will find a pattern in their responses. If we tend to think through our values, then we are likely to think through most of our values. If we tend to go by social norms, we can expect that to have influenced many of our values. My colleague found all of his values to be shaped from personal intuition; in addition, he had trouble listing very many values.

SUMMARY

No two individuals have the same set of experiences no matter how closely they have lived together or how much their lives or careers parallel each other. Every person takes a different journey through life and the nature of that journey shapes who we are. In this chapter, I suggested listing significant experiences—those incidents that have had a profound and meaningful influence on the way we are. In order to better understand or deepen our appreciation of those events, I proposed we question how we came to see them as significant and why we care about them. The process by which we come to name something as significant tells us about ourselves. The premise upon which we base our perception of significance in our lives is at the center of self-knowledge.

Although our values are often derived from our experiences and from our basic sense of Self, it is conducive to a good self-awareness to separate the threads of our values from the general fabric of our experience and nature. In the second part of this chapter, I presented a process for identifying and questioning our values. Again, I believe it is important to consider how we came to hold the values we do and why they are important to us.

CHAPTER 3

The Good Teacher

The literature presents us with a bewildering array of characteristics of good teaching. Any person trying to measure up to all of these qualities and traits will inevitably fall short on several dimensions. We are told that good teachers are organized and spontaneous, caring and critical, structured and flexible, calm and enthusiastic, challenging and supportive, firm and empathic, warm and disciplined, collaborative and questioning, reflective and charismatic, practical and innovative, creative and down-to-earth, and open and directive. In addition, of course, they are experts in the subject area in which they teach, keep up to date with current trends in their field, are socially aware, see themselves as responsible for social change, are involved in the community, and are models for their students. If they teach at a research university, they are also actively involved in the pursuit of new knowledge in their discipline through well-funded research projects, and their research informs their teaching practice. It hardly needs to be mentioned that good teachers also plan programs, write curriculum, serve on committees, engage in professional development activities, have input into political issues related to education, and are advocates of the importance of quality teaching at their institutions.

In trying to be everything a good teacher is supposed to be, we cannot be ourselves. A split occurs between Teacher and Self. We see ourselves as playing roles; we experience feelings of inferiority and failure; we become exhausted and stressed under the burden of attempting to be all things, and especially all things to all students. In this chapter, I review four kinds of good teaching. I do not believe there are only four kinds of good teachers; however, I think the categories I have chosen represent themes in the literature as well as illustrate how different good teachers can be. I briefly trace the theoretical origins of each category and point out some of the contradictions between them. I argue that each kind of teaching has its place and is not ideal in every context. I go on to illustrate how good teaching finds its place by presenting two short scenarios and suggest an exercise for teachers to reflect on their own personal style.

THE ORGANIZED TEACHER

The organized teacher displays this quality in relation to both content and process. The content of the course is clearly structured, and the relationships among topics are explicitly laid out. There is a clear course outline, objectives, and strategies for evaluating student learning that are in line with the objectives. A sequence is established so that prerequisite learning carefully precedes the more advanced topics. The process followed is similarly organized. Each class has explicit objectives. The purpose of the session is stated at the beginning or perhaps displayed on an overhead transparency. The class may be linked to previous classes. Regardless of the teaching strategies used, the agenda proceeds on time and comes to a closure that foreshadows the next session.

The emphasis on organization in teaching has its origins in behavioral psychology. Beginning in the late 1800s, early psychologists such as Thorndike and Watson experimented with the stimulus-response connection that determined the direction of the psychology of learning for at least 40 years (Hilgard & Bower, 1966). B. F. Skinner (see, for example, Skinner, 1953) shaped our views of teaching for a good part of this century. It was felt that if learning were broken into small enough steps and a reward system carefully designed, anybody could learn just about anything. Programmed instruction, modularized instruction, early computer-assisted instruction, and what was then known as "educational technology" or instructional design were based on this premise. A strong organization is the foundation of the behaviorist approach to teaching. What behaviorism does not do is take into account the person, the cognitive and affective processes within the student.

Instructional design originated with the United States military in the 1940s and became a common method for writing curriculum and preparing programs in all facets of education over the following decades. It consists of a systematic procedure for the development of learning materials. A needs assessment may be used to determine what students already know about a subject area. Behavioral objectives (in which the product of the learning must be observable) specify the learning that will take place. Sometimes, a distinction is made between terminal or final objectives and enabling objectives—those which lead to the terminal objectives. Task or procedural analysis is used to determine the optimal sequencing of instruction: objectives are carefully analyzed to determine which segments of learning must precede others. Teaching materials and techniques are studied in terms of the requirements of the task as outlined in the objectives. Evaluation of learning follows directly from the objectives which already specify the outcome or product of the learning.

It is easy to see how an emphasis on instructional design leads to well-organized teaching. Whether or not it is appropriate for teaching in all domains of knowledge and in all contexts is a question we need to reflect on. When the knowledge is instrumental or technical in nature, behavioral objectives and task analyses may well be helpful for both teachers and students, but when we are working with communicative (understanding others) or emancipatory (increased self-awareness) knowledge, I seriously question the need for a technical approach to teaching. Just as important, or perhaps even more so, is our own style, nature, values, and preferences as teachers.

Being organized is not a bad thing. Students certainly appreciate a clear course outline, a well-planned class, and explicit links among the topics in a course. But organization can also interfere with good teaching. Brookfield (1990, pp. 58–59) reminds us that "learning is not a rational, bloodless ascetic phenomenon." In adjusting teaching to the rhythms of learning,

Brookfield suggests we need to recognize emotionality, adapt to fluctuations in the learning process, build on the unexpected, and consider learning styles. Pushing ahead in order to stick to the agenda, cover the material, and stay organized is not always what the moment needs.

THE CARING TEACHER

The caring teacher centers himself on the student as person. He is concerned with establishing a warm and friendly atmosphere in the classroom, providing support, encouraging good relationships among students, and making sure the needs and feelings of each individual are considered. He genuinely and empathically listens. He goes out of his way, gives up his own time, and takes those extra steps to ensure students are comfortable in their learning experience. The caring teacher avoids being an authority figure or a disciplinarian. The person and the process the person is engaged in is valued as much as, if not more than, the content and structure of the discipline.

The notion of the caring teacher has its origins in humanism, though caring teachers are often simply caring people who have gone into teaching—it is not that they have read somewhere that they should be caring. In philosophy, humanism has a variety of meanings, including the movement that characterized the culture of the Renaissance where human achievements and possibilities were celebrated. In psychology, humanism grew out of the work of Abraham Maslow and Carl Rogers. Maslow (1968) rejected behaviorism as too narrow and advocated humanism—a concern with self-realization, higher human motives, and aesthetic needs. Rogers (1951, 1969) developed a "self theory of personality" based on his client-centered, nondirective therapy. He assumes an individual can understand himself given the right conditions. He believes that the most basic human drive is to actualize, to maintain and enhance the Self.

Humanism is the foundation of much of adult education in which an emphasis is placed on providing support for adults who presumably are anxious and lacking in self-confidence after being away from a school setting for a number of years or are oppressed due to social conditions. Humanism has had less influence in higher education, where the discipline or subject area tends to take precedence over the personal needs of the student. Yet, the research and literature in higher education also underlines the importance of collaboration, building trust with students, and considering individual differences among students (for example, Beckman, 1990, Chickering & Gamson, 1991, Fiechtner & Davis, 1992). Almost every student rating form for the evaluation of teaching has a cluster of items related to caring for students. Statistical analyses of student ratings of instruction nearly always yield a factor to do with rapport with students and facilitating relationships among students. It is clear that the caring teacher is valued.

Indeed, we want caring teachers, and we want to be caring teachers. Who would argue otherwise? But what happens when caring comes into conflict with other aspects of teaching? We feel guilty when we challenge students rather than support them, or when we cannot give a student or a class what they want, or when we simply do not like a student. If we value organization or structure, or see it as important for a particular subject area, can we simultaneously work to meet the needs of all individuals in the course? Can we be both caring and organized? Although we always want to remain caring teachers, there are times when we do not exclusively focus on the student as person.

THE PRACTICAL TEACHER

The practical teacher is down-to-earth and realistic. She works with real experiences and real objects. She brings specimens and models into the classroom and takes her students on field trips so they can see what is really going on. Students have no doubt as to how they can use the information presented and the material covered in the course. Rather than reading about things or talking about abstract ideas, students are engaged in doing, building, and discovering. They solve real-life problems and can see the relevance of doing so. The practical teacher has a large repertoire of pragmatic examples and illustrations. She relates learning to the daily lives of her students and to what is going on in the world outside of the classroom.

The value we place on practical teaching is most commonly seen as having its origins in the work of John Dewey, though we could trace it to other sources as well. John Dewey was an American philosopher, educator and psychologist writing in the late 1800s and early 1900s. He founded the functionalist movement in psychology, based on instrumentalistic philosophy. He described ideas as plans for action that arise in response to a problem. Merriam and Brockett (1997, p. 35) describe John Dewey as the "most eloquent and widely known advocate for the application of pragmatism to education." Among Dewey's influential books are *Education and Democracy* (1916), *How We Think* (1933), and *Experience and Education* (1938). In large part, it was Dewey's work that led to a broader view of education (going beyond liberal education), a focus on learners and their needs and experiences, the use of problem-solving activities and experience-based approaches in teaching, and a shift away from the teacher as authority figure.

Today, we talk about experiential learning. Experiential learning is so pervasive in educational thinking, theory, and practice, that it has almost moved beyond questioning and critique. Kolb's model of experiential learning and its accompanying popular Learning Style Inventory (Kolb, 1984) has helped to increase all educators' awareness of the value of this approach. Kolb describes a learning cycle in which we participate in a concrete experience, engage in reflection observation on the experience, form an abstract conceptualization or theory that helps us to understand the experience, and actively experiment with the theory to solve practical problems.

In higher education, we find more criticism of experiential learning than elsewhere, especially from traditional scholars who do not see the goal of higher education as catering to the practical needs of business and industry. Some see experiential learning as having a special place in higher education, such as in teacher education and educational technology (Bassett & Jackson, 1994) or in any field-based academic programs that incorporate internships and practicums (Lewis & Williams, 1994). But in addition to this, experiential learning activities in the classroom, in the form of case studies, role playing, and simulations, are widely advocated (Cranton, 1998b; Davis, 1993).

We want and expect teaching to be practical. The slogan, "learn by doing," is familiar to educators at all levels. In adult education especially, it is hardly questioned that we consider the role of experience as central even though the research on the effectiveness of experiential learning is sparse. Is it always best to be practical? By focusing on the here-and-now, do we risk overlooking innovation and visions of the future. By accentuating the concrete, do we miss the abstract? By emphasizing the details, do we lose the big picture? Can we do all of these things simultaneously? If it is in our nature to be visionary, can we also be practical?

THE CREATIVE TEACHER

The creative teacher sees teaching as an opportunity to change things, to bring about improvements, and to work with visions of the future. He infuses his classes with his enthusiasm and intensity. He initiates, promotes, and speculates. He inspires students to tackle new and difficult learning tasks. The creative teacher kindles excitement for the subject area, rarely does the same thing the same way twice, and constantly experiments with new teaching methods and new approaches to his discipline.

Creativity originally came to be of interest to educators through the work of Guilford (1950, 1959) who was deeply dissatisfied with the traditional definitions and measurements of intelligence. He devised a *structure of intellect* model in which he distinguished between five intellectual operations: cognition, memory, convergent thinking, divergent thinking, and evaluation. Convergent thinking is closed-system thinking, that which yields good answers to traditional intelligence tests. Divergent thinking is creative—thinking in different directions, searching, and seeking variety. A considerable amount of work was done in the 1960s on creativity, primarily attempts to define and measure it. Familiar names from that time include Torrance (1962, 1963) and Hudson (1968). Later, in the 1970s, De Bono's (1970) work on lateral thinking became popular and was used extensively in professional development workshops and seminars. Creative thinking now tends to be integrated into models of critical thinking. Brookfield (1991), for example, lists the characteristics of creativity he sees as part of thinking critically: rejecting standardized formats for problem solving, having divergent interests, taking multiple perspectives on a problem, viewing the world as relative and contextual, using trial-and-error methods, having a future-orientation, and having self-confidence.

Many of our current views of cognitive development place creative characteristics at the upper developmental levels (for example, see King & Kitchener, 1994). Moving beyond rational to extrarational, imaginative, or intuitive learning is also a new perspective on creativity in teaching and learning (for example, see Clark, 1997; Dirkx, 1997). It is clear that we are putting a high value on creativity, but perhaps in a difference sense than did Guilford many decades ago. Saying that someone's work is rational, linear, or sequential can now be interpreted as an insult, in some circles at least.

We need creative teachers, especially as our social and technological world becomes increasingly complex and full of change. The visionary teacher may be valued above all others as we embark on a new century. And what if this is not our strength? What if you and I are people who integrate, organize, and systematize rather than think in all directions simultaneously? Shall we try to be whom we are not? Perhaps the creative mind is not best for every teaching context. Perhaps there is also a place for order and attention to detail.

A PLACE FOR ALL GOOD TEACHERS

When people describe their teaching weaknesses, they usually describe the flip side of their strengths. They see themselves as a bad teacher because they do not do the opposite of what they do well. Being the good teacher sometimes means that we are, at the same time, a bad teacher as we are not doing the opposite of what we are doing. In my twenty years of experience as a faculty developer, I have so often heard people dismiss what they do well in teaching and explain why they are poor teachers.

Ralph teaches leadership and organizational behavior. He is energetic and innovative. His enthusiasm for his subject area is catching—students find themselves drawn into learning regardless of their initial motivation for attending one of Ralph's courses. Students work primarily in groups, but Ralph goes from group to group, teasing, talking, and giving mini-lectures on the topics of discussion. The students often accuse Ralph of interrupting their work, but they enjoy his presence. Ralph rarely teaches a course in the same way twice in a row. He is continually experimenting with new approaches to the subject area and to teaching strategies. Ralph's classes are rather haphazard at times, and he worries about this. No matter how hard he tries, he doesn't seem to be able to stay with an agenda. There are just too many interesting things to pursue. If a topic does not get finished, he just goes on with it the following week. Some students feel lost and wish there could be just a little more structure. Ralph also enjoys challenging students, pushing them beyond the limits of what they normally do. He sometimes gives caustic remarks on assignments and he encourages the groups to compete against each other. The quieter and gentler souls in his class sometimes wish he would be more supportive and understanding.

Frances is a chemistry teacher. She describes her first goal in teaching as fostering a love for science in her classroom. Frances pays a great deal of attention to individual students and makes sure she gets to know everyone, even when this means she spends an inordinate number of hours meeting with students outside of class. She is genuinely interested in her students' personal lives, commitments, and problems. Frances understands that many students struggle with science and are intimidated by the technical problems they work with in the laboratory. She does everything she can to ease their learning. As a result, in most semesters, Frances has difficulty getting through the course outline as it is given in the departmental program. Her colleagues tell her she must cover more material; they don't want to be making up for Frances's poor teaching when her students go on into their courses. "If you would spend as much time teaching as you do listening to their sob stories," a colleague said, "your students would learn a lot more chemistry." Frances worries about this a great deal. She suspects her colleagues might be right, but then, she wonders, how can the students learn anything when they are scared stiff or overwhelmed by personal problems.

Should Ralph curtail his enthusiasm and creativity in order to be better organized? Or can he keep his personal style and add a layer of structure over it? Should Frances spend less time caring about students and more time teaching material? Would she be a better teacher? Can she compromise, spending just a little less time caring and a little more time pushing people through the course so that they have covered all the topics?

I am not arguing that we should use our personal preferences, styles, or values as a rationalization for neglecting important aspects of teaching. But neither should we neglect or suppress our preferences in order to meet someone else's standards of good teaching. The authentic teacher understands who she is as a teacher, works well and clearly with her own style, and continues to reflect on her practice, grow, and develop. Ralph may well find ways to give a little more structure for those students who need it; Frances may volunteer to help restructure the courses in the program so that her introductory course need not include as much material. But Ralph should not give up his unique and creative approaches, and neither should Frances try to stop caring so much for individual students.

In one of my classrooms, students designed and put up a large poster. It depicted a cartoon-style drawing of a dog—white with large black spots. The caption read, "Everyone needs a Spot." The group that summer was concerned with everyone having a place, a way of being that represented their own individuality as well as a way of belonging to the group as a whole.

How can we find our spot as teachers? How can we determine our personal teaching preferences and strengths? In Chapters 1 and 2, I suggest reflection on who we are, our psychological preferences, our experiences, and our values. With the results of these exercises in mind, the next step is to contemplate what we value in teaching, how we have come to hold those values, and why they are important to us.

In Exercise 3.1, I present a series of questions which can be used as a guide to thinking about the ways in which we are good teachers.

The first part of Exercise 3.1 contains a series of statements which may help identify our teaching strengths. The more checks in each category, the more likely this is a preferred teaching style or a way of teaching at which we excel. Equally as important as identifying what we do well is contemplating how this came to be (process reflection) and why it is important to us (premise reflection). The questions in Part Two and Part Three of the exercise are intended to guide reflection.

For example, Marcia, an English teacher at a community college has the following scores:

Organized=5
Caring=2
Practical=0
Creative=3

She identifies strongly with the description of the organized teacher, but worries that she is "too organized," not flexible enough. She has difficulty relating her subject matter to her students' lives and thinks this may cause problems for many students. "It seems I can never just come up with a good example on the spot, as my colleagues do," she worries.

When Marcia reflected on the questions in Part Two of the exercise, she decided she was an organized teacher because she was an organized person. "This is the way I run my whole life,"

Exercise 3.1 Finding Your Spot

Part One: Teaching Strengths. Check off the statements that describe you as a teacher.

A. ____ I make good and clear decisions about my teaching.
B. ____ I consider the needs and feelings of each student.
C. ____ I encourage students to learn by doing.
D. ____ I am continually trying out new things in my teaching.
E. ____ I always stick with my agenda.
F. ____ If a student needs help, I would abandon my agenda.
G. ____ I am more down-to-earth than innovative in my teaching.
H. ____ I get bored with teaching if I do it the same way twice.
I. ____ I have a clear objective and structure for each class.
J. ____ I set up a warm and friendly atmosphere in my classroom.
K. ____ I give good concrete examples of every concept.
L. ____ I am charismatic and enthusiastic.
M. ____ I clarify relationships among topics in each class.
N. ____ I genuinely and empathically listen to students.
O. ____ I work with real experiences and real objects in teaching.
P. ____ I challenge students to develop visions of the future.
Q. ____ I plan each class carefully in advance.
R. ____ I am a teacher primarily because I like to help others.
S. ____ I prefer teaching facts and information.
T. ____ I like to speculate about the new and unknown in class.

Count the number of check marks you have in each category:

Organized (A + E + I + M + Q) = _____
Caring   (B + F + J + N + R) = _____
Practical (C + G + K + O + S) = _____
Creative   (D + H + L + P + T) = _____

Part Two.   How did I come to have these strengths?

Did I deliberately and consciously develop these strengths?
Are my teaching strengths related to my caring for people?
Are my teaching strengths based on my past experiences?
Do these strengths represent my vision of good teaching?

Part Three.   Why do these strengths matter?

Do they matter because they can be objectively and rationally justified?
Do they matter because they bring pleasure to others and fit the social norms of good teaching?
Do they matter because experience has taught me they work?
Do they matter because of the reform and change I can bring about if I teach this way?

---

she commented, "not just my classroom." She did see herself as deliberately developing organizational skills in teaching, but this was because it "suited" her, it fit with the way she saw herself in general. "I can't *not* be organized," she said, "so I just kept doing more of what I do best."

In Part Three of the exercise, Marcia wondered whether organization mattered at all. She could justify it, yes, but she thought it might be better to focus on something else in her development.

When I worked with Marcia to help her come up with a developmental plan, we focused on using her strength in organizing to tackle other areas that interested her. Rather than trying to be "less organized," which would go against her nature, Marcia created a well-organized developmental plan. She decided to prepare concrete examples as a part of her planning for each class. If she had examples already selected, Marcia felt she could incorporate them into her class in an appropriate way. She even planned to be more flexible: she deliberately left free time in each class, and she planned several options from which she could choose depending on how the class was going. Marcia felt very positive about this approach rather than frustrated as she had been when she simply tried to be less structured in her practice.

SUMMARY

There is no one way to be a good teacher (see Cranton, 1998b, for example). No research has shown teachers with certain characteristics are consistently more effective than teachers with other characteristics. If we knew such a thing, it would certainly make life easier for those who hire teachers or work in faculty development, but fortunately, a great variety of people are good teachers. From the charismatic, extraverted, dynamic lecturer to the quiet, calm, thoughtful facilitator, each person has something to offer the teaching profession.

There may well be people who are not cut out to be teachers, for whatever reason. I think most such people realize this and do not become teachers in the first place, or gravitate to other roles after a short period of time. I do not intend to imply that every person is equally likely to be an excellent teacher. The nature of the work suits some better than others.

On the other hand, and this is the central point I want to make in this chapter, I think that anyone who is a practicing teacher in higher education can become a better teacher by becoming an authentic teacher—by teaching in a way that is true to her Self. We are told that it is good to be organized, caring, practical, and creative. Each of these perspectives on teaching has clear roots in varying schools of thought in education and psychology. Each is valid in that a community of theorists and scholars has come to consensus on its validity. But knowledge of teaching is communicative in nature, and hence there is no absolute truth, no one right way of being. No person can be all things that different communities of scholars have deigned good teaching to be. This, unfortunately though, is what our literature on effective teaching has come to. All perspectives are simultaneously seen to be true. Practicing teachers twirl around like whirlwinds trying to be all perspectives at once.

In this chapter, I described the organized teacher, the caring teacher, the practical teacher, and the creative teacher, situating each in its theoretical context. I suggested that we each, individually, find our own place within these perspectives through questioning, contemplation, and reflection on our basic nature, preferences, experience, and values.

CHAPTER 4

Self As Teacher, Teacher As Self

So often, we see teaching as playing a role, putting on a performance, being other than who we are. In the literature, we read about the many roles we can and should play as teachers. Strategies, techniques, and tips are prescribed. In popular films such as *Mr. Holland's Opus* and *Good-bye Mr. Chips*, we find the image of teacher as larger than life. Being human, we tend to take the gifts we have for granted and to admire and try to adopt the characteristics and roles that are unlike us. What is your image of the ideal teacher? How many of the characteristics of your ideal teacher do you possess? Do you try to act out the part of an ideal teacher?

I recently discussed the idea of being an authentic teacher with a seasoned science education professor—a man who was looking forward to retirement within the next year after thirty years of teaching practice. He was almost appalled at the notion of being oneself with students. "I don't think I could go for that," he said, startled by what he saw as my naivety. "Who I am in the classroom and who I am outside of the classroom are two different people. Students don't need to know *me*, they need to know how to teach science." Perhaps my raising the topic provoked images of personal self-disclosure or an emotional sharing of feelings with students, things that had no place in his mind in science teaching, but more likely, he simply saw teaching as something he does rather than who he is.

Heimlich and Norland (1994) describe a teacher fashion show they held. Participants created and acted out an image of an ideal teacher based on a piece of prescriptive writing. When they used costumes, props, gestures, and descriptions to stereotype and caricature the writing, the nature of the "ideal" became obvious—something that no one could or would want to be. As teachers, how can we be ourselves?

Brookfield (1990) proposes that being an authentic teacher includes making sure our behaviors are congruent with our words, admitting we do not have all the answers and can make mistakes, building trust with students through revealing personal aspects of ourselves and our experiences, and respecting students as people. These are undoubtedly good things to do in order to be authentic, but I believe there is more we can to do bring our Self into our teaching, to merge Self and Teacher. Teaching is about people communicating and working together toward a common goal. Doing this well requires bringing ourselves as human beings into the relationship. Working together comes only if we know one another.

In this chapter, I first suggest we examine our own stories—how we came to be teachers and who we are as teachers. Second, I present a process for contemplating the *teacher within* ourselves, those aspects of our personality, values, and background that are congruent with our expectations of an ideal teacher. Third, I propose we consider the *teacher without*, those characteristics of Teacher we see in others but not in ourselves. Finally, I offer some thoughts on how Self and Teacher might be merged.

OUR STORY

Although stories have been used throughout human history as a way of understanding ourselves and our context, it is only fairly recently that the power of narrative is being recognized as both a teaching and learning tool and as a means of understanding our own development as teachers. Bruner (1986) sees holistic thinkers—those people who cognitively process the large picture, global concepts, and groups of concepts—as using narrative thinking. MacKeracher (1996, p. 107) depicts narrative thinking as a "useful way to store and describe information for which no clearly defined propositional knowledge is available."

She advocates narratives as a way of examining our sense of self and self-esteem. Connelly and Clandinin (1994) encourage teachers to tell their stories, pointing out that the telling of a new story is often the retelling of a past story. With each telling, the story becomes richer and new meaning emerges.

In developing as teachers, we need not only to link theory to practice, or use theory to increase our repertoire of practical knowledge, but also to connect both to our personal experience. As van Halen-Faber (1997) points out in her description of using narrative in preservice teacher education, when we add the word "person" to concepts such as *knowledge, relevance, responsibility,* and *voice*, each concept shifts from a value-neutral position to a value-laden one. We have *personal knowledge, personal relevance, personal responsibility,* and *personal voice.* Knowledge about teaching is primarily constructivist in nature, putting the emphasis on the person—the person who is the teacher and the person who is the learner.

Storytelling helps us to establish "general themes that typify a single human life seen in its full social context" (Miller, 1991, p. 64). In order to be authentic—true to ourselves—in our teaching practice, we need to tell and retell our story as teacher. Finding new meaning in our stories demonstrates how critical reflection enhances narrative. In Exercise 4.1, I offer some guidelines for telling our story of being a teacher.

I suggest that the story actually be told, not simply thought about. Telling may take the form of writing—in prose, outline form, or even in poetry or a play for those so gifted. The advantage of putting the story down on paper is that it can be revisited and revised. For individuals who regularly keep teaching journals or personal journals, these provide an excellent resource and basis for reflection. However, it may feel more natural for some people to tell their story to another person. In this case, audio- or videotaping it may be worth considering. Following Gardner's (1993) notion of multiple intelligences, some teachers may prefer to depict their story through drawing, painting, photographs, music, dance or movement, a scrapbook, or some combination of these.

In whatever way we choose to express the story, the process

Exercise 4.1 Telling Your Story

Consider as many of the following questions as seem to be relevant to telling your story. Before dismissing a question as not relevant, spend a few moments seeing if you can find a place for it, or some version of it, in relating your experiences.

1. As a child and adolescent, what was your view of teachers?
2. What was the view of teachers in the community or culture where you grew up?
3. When did you first think that you might become a teacher?
4. How did your view of teachers change as you went on to higher education?
5. Are there teachers in your family?
6. Did you deliberately choose to become a teacher or did you "fall into it?"
7. Did you have friends in childhood or young adulthood who wanted to become teachers?
8. What was your very first teaching experience either in an informal or a formal setting?
9. How did you feel about your early teaching experiences?
10. What aspects of yourself make you a natural teacher? (For example, do you like to help others, want to improve the world you live in, like explaining things?)
11. What critical incidents changed your view of teaching?
12. Which teachers do you admire, either from your past or present experience?
13. Do you currently have friends or family members who are also teachers?
14. What kinds of things do you do in order to grow and develop as a teacher?
15. How would you describe your relationships with students? How have these relationships changed over time?

16. What aspects of your personality, values, or beliefs do you *not* take into the classroom with you?

17. What are the major ways in which you are different as a teacher now as compared to when you first started teaching?

---

of pulling teaching experiences together into a narrative will foster critical self-reflection and bring new insights into understanding our Self as Teacher.

Reflection on some or all of these questions and "telling the story" helps us to understand the Self that is Teacher. Virleen Carlson (personal communication, 1999), a faculty developer from Cornell University, writes,

> I taught in a high school setting for 15 years and "became" a "J" personality [judgmental, following Jung's psychological type theory] because the culture demanded it. . . . It was only when I went through a Ph.D. program and started to work here at Cornell (reading quite a bit) that I realized my personality was in antithesis to my teaching style. For example, I had been told that students should come into class on time, whereas my authentic nature really doesn't care. Once I tuned into a more authentic teaching style, I now know which things really matter to me as a teacher (honesty, values, learning), and which I can let go of.

THE TEACHER WITHIN

Becoming an authentic teacher involves, in part understanding those aspects of oneself that are in harmony with teaching. What do we do in everyday life outside of the classroom that is teaching or related to teaching? Help our children grow and develop? Contribute to community or social groups? Organize community events? Show a friend how to bake something or grow flowers? Care for and train a pet? In order to see Self as Teacher, or see the teacher within ourselves, we need to continually walk back and forth over the artificial line drawn between "in the classroom" and "out of the classroom," or "at school" and "at home" until the line hardly exists.

Apps (1996) tells us that "teaching from the heart means teaching from the depths of who we are with the hope that we will touch the hearts of those with whom we work" (p. 63), and also that "there is risk when you teach from your heart, because you begin touching the core of who you are" (p. 110). Being an authentic teacher means involving your full Self in your work.

When I posed a question to members of the Professional and Organizational Development (POD) network on how they saw authentic teaching, the response was overwhelming. Caryn Berg from the Department of Anthropology at the University of Colorado put it well when she responded,

> I definitely believe we should let our real selves show through in our teaching. I think students respond better to teachers whom they see as real people with lives of their own. I can think of a million times when I have started out the class by telling students about my weekend or an upcoming event . . . They are more apt to ask questions and share themselves in classroom discussions when they are comfortable with you as a person . . . I actually think it enhances our ability to control classroom situations and help students learn. (personal communication, 1999)

How can we find the teacher that is naturally within ourselves and bring her into our interactions with students? Brookfield (1995) suggests that our autobiographies represent one important source of insight, but he cautions that with this and other approaches to private self-reflection we cannot completely avoid denial and distortion. We may be "trapped in" our own perspectives and need to check our understanding with others or against the literature. Discovering "one's authentic voice is at the heart of the critically reflective process," and "the realization of the power of one's own authentic voice is a beautiful thing to experience" (Brookfield, 1995, p. 47).

In Exercise 4.2, I propose one way of finding the teacher within ourselves, or our authentic voice as a teacher. The first part of the exercise involves identifying the aspects of our Self in everyday life that also match our notion of the ideal teacher. Following Brookfield's advice, in the second part of the exercise, I suggest validating this list with a student, former student, colleague, or anyone else who knows us as teachers.

Exercise 4.2 Finding the Teacher Within

Part One:

Consider the way you are and the things you typically do on a weekend, a holiday, at home, or any other occasion when you are not teaching. Think about how you are with family, friends, or in social groups outside of your teaching environment. List as many **adjectives** (for example, caring, funny, calm, relaxed, adventuresome) as you can that describe yourself in these contexts.

_____	_____	_____
_____	_____	_____
_____	_____	_____

Now list as many **verbs** (for example, talk, laugh, create, read) as you can that describe what you do in these contexts.

_____	_____	_____
_____	_____	_____
_____	_____	_____

Next, think about or visualize an ideal teacher. Which of the adjectives and verbs you have listed would also be characteristics of an ideal teacher? List those below.

_____	_____	_____
_____	_____	_____
_____	_____	_____
_____	_____	_____

Part Two:

Meet with a student, former student, colleague, or anyone else who knows you in your teaching context. The person should know you fairly well and should also be someone whom you like and trust. Give that person your first two lists—the adjectives and verbs—and ask him or her to check off those that describe you and what you do.

If we examine carefully who we are as people, consider ourselves in life outside of teaching, we inevitably find the characteristics we bring to teaching. Teaching is not a technical skill—it is not something we do in a certain environment with a certain set of machines or tools. Teaching is communicative—involving a knowledge of others and social norms—and emancipatory—involving increased self-understanding. It centers on relationships and therefore involves us fully as persons. As Apps (1996, p. 9) puts it, "education is a series of relationships: learners relating to their own intellectual, emotional, physical, and spiritual selves; teachers relating to learners; learners relating to each other; learners relating to knowledge; and teachers and learners relating to contexts and communities."

THE TEACHER WITHOUT

Just as there are aspects of our character we can bring naturally from our everyday life into teaching, there are aspects of teaching that are not a part of how we are. As I point out in Chapter 3, there are innumerable lists of teaching qualities, covering every possible facet of human nature. We cannot ever be all of those things. There are teachers we know, including excellent teachers, who are outside of the realm of how *we* can be. This is what I mean by *the teacher without*—the teacher we are not. When we try to imitate the teacher without, we are inauthentic.

Brookfield (1995) vividly describes what he calls the imposter syndrome. "We wear an external mask of control, but beneath it we know that really we are frail figures . . . [A]round the corner is an unforeseen but cataclysmic event that will reveal us as frauds" (p. 230). Lieberman and Miller (1991) also underline the uncertainties, fears, and lack of confidence among teachers in their discussion of professional development for educators. There is no safe place, they suggest, for teachers to talk about their doubts. Teaching is, rather oddly, considered a private matter. I propose that teachers feel like frauds, at least in part, under the influence of the teacher without.

Unlike some other professionals or people working the trades, for example, teachers have experienced a wide variety of teaching. As learners, they have experienced a minimum of 16 years of working with teachers. No automobile mechanic has experienced being a car under the hands of different mechanics. Teachers have studied theory and read practical prescriptive texts. In an area where there are no right answers—no one way—there is scope for a tremendous number of answers and ways. We cannot be all of these people or do all of these things. We feel like imposters.

Brookfield (1995) suggests dealing with or controlling the imposter syndrome by making it public through peer teaching, talking with colleagues informally, and engaging in discussion groups. He also sees a positive side to feeling like an imposter— it keeps us on our toes, encourages us to critically reflect on our practice, and prevents us from becoming complacent. Perhaps, though, there are better motivators to develop our teaching than feeling fearful, insecure, and vulnerable. I would prefer that we uncover the basis for the imposter syndrome by examining who it is we think we should be.

In Exercise 4.3, I offer one strategy for delineating the teacher we are not. First, we need to think of exactly what it is we do not do. Rather than maintaining a vague, abstract concept of the ideal teacher we will never be, we can pin it down. Who is this person? What, precisely, do they do? When we have such a list, we can ask whether these are things we could develop, or whether they are antithetical to our very nature. If the characteristics are not within our character, we need to look at the flip side of them and align ourselves with the strength represented there. With the exception of immoral or cruel behaviors, there are few flip sides that cannot also be interpreted as teaching strengths. If I see effervescence as a good quality of the teacher without, the flip side may be calmness, a peaceful, quiet nature. A calm, peaceful, quiet teacher can be perceived as a great treasure by students.

People who complete this exercise find two benefits. First, they identify in a concrete fashion those characteristics and behaviors they do not have but think are ideal—the things that

Exercise 4.3 Finding the Teacher Without

Part One:

Contemplate your images or ideas of ideal teachers. Focus on the qualities they have that you do **not** have. List as many **adjectives** (for example, organized, charismatic, dedicated, funny) as you can that describe characteristics of the ideal teacher but do **not** describe you.

_____	_____	_____
_____	_____	_____
_____	_____	_____

Now list as many **verbs** (for example, challenge, question, support, stimulate) as you can that describe what the ideal teacher does but you do **not** do.

_____	_____	_____
_____	_____	_____
_____	_____	_____

Of those verbs and adjectives you have listed, ask which ones you could develop while remaining true to your nature and which are completely counter to your nature. List those that are counter to your nature here.

_____	_____	_____
_____	_____	_____
_____	_____	_____

Part Two:

Examine your third list, those adjectives and verbs which are antithetic to your character. List the **opposite** of each word here.

_____	_____	_____
_____	_____	_____
_____	_____	_____

Finally, if any of these words have a negative connotation for you, find another, parallel word that does not sound negative. For example, if you have listed "cold" as the opposite of "caring," you may find "crisp" or "proud" or "efficient" to be better words. List the alternatives here.

_____	_____	_____
_____	_____	_____
_____	_____	_____

make them feel like imposters. Second, for almost every characteristic or behavior teachers list, they find its opposite does describe them, and this opposite has a facet that is a strength. Separating the teacher without from the teacher within ourselves allows us to place Self and Teacher in harmony with each other.

MERGING OF SELF AND TEACHER

Most developmental psychologists, Tennant and Pogson (1995) point out, portray development as including a strengthening of the self in relation to the power of social forces. As we mature both professionally and personally, we are able to separate who we are from who others think we should be or who our culture or community expects us to be. Jung's ([1921] 1971) concept of individuation provides a good psychological framework for this notion. As we form our identity, a lifelong process, we continually differentiate ourselves from the collective of humanity. Sharp (1995) writes that "without such consciousness, one is doomed to remain dependent and imitative, feeling misunderstood and suppressed, unwittingly victimized by a collectively acceptable persona" (pp. 75–76). Perhaps this is another way of viewing the imposter syndrome. Becoming an authentic teacher involves knowing who we are and expressing our true Self in our work.

As teachers, we need to differentiate ourselves from the collective community of teachers and form both our sense of Self as Teacher as well as how the collective sense of teacher is a part

of our Self. Tennant and Pogson (1995) point out the paradoxical quality of this process—of being separate while being at-
tached. Yet, as Sharp (1995) says, we cannot develop unless we
choose our own way, consciously and with moral deliberation.
The development of the personality means "fidelity to the law
of one's own being," "the segregation of the individual from the
undifferentiated and unconscious herd," and this means isolation (p. 48).

Brookfield (1995) describes this sense of isolation as cultural suicide: "Cultural suicide happens when people who make
public their questioning of taken-for-granted assumptions and
expectations find themselves excluded from the culture that has
defined and sustained them up to that point in their lives" (p.
236). He suggests a variety of strategies for minimizing cultural
suicide or the isolation we feel when we differentiate ourselves
from the collective community of teachers in order to find our
own path. The strategies focus primarily on reassuring colleagues that you continue to respect their expertise and experience while finding a small group or even one like-minded person. The latter suggestion fits well with Jung's ([1921] 1971)
notion that as we individuate, we find new groups that better
meet our emerging sense of Self.

How can we merge Self and Teacher? Teacher is a socially
constructed concept. Self, we find within. Yet a part of how we
see ourselves is also bound to what we do, to teaching. What I
have tried to do in the sections on the teacher within and the
teacher without is to take the construct of *teacher* and separate
out which aspects of it are a part of our true sense of Self and
which are a part of the collective concept of teaching, but not
related to our individual identity.

When we merge Teacher and Self to express ourselves authentically, we need to work with those facets of the construct
of *teacher* that are congruent with our sense of Self. Otherwise,
we lose our sense of Self, become frustrated trying to be someone else, and feel like a fraud, an imposter.

Although we each need to find our own strategies for merg-
ing our sense of Self into teaching, some of the following suggestions may be a starting point.

- Monitor yourself. If you are exhausted after teaching or stressed before teaching, it may be because you are putting energy into maintaining an inauthentic role.
- Keep a journal. Divide the journal into two halves, either on each page or separate pages. Write about your teaching and write about your life outside of teaching. Periodically review your journal with an eye out for discrepancies in your thinking, experiences, and feelings.
- Find a colleague or a small group of colleagues whom you see as authentic teachers. Talk about authentic teaching. Exchange stories. Visit each other's classes if this is practical.
- Videotape your teaching and scrutinize the videotape for actions that seem inauthentic.
- Ask your students to point out occasions when they see you as "faking it." Make this into a game or a regular feedback exercise. It may be important to allow students to provide comments anonymously, at least initially until they trust your reactions and understand what you are doing.
- Experiment with different teaching strategies and methods in order to find those that are most comfortable for you as a person.
- Consult the literature on teaching (for example, Cranton, 1998b; Heimlich and Norland, 1994), looking for styles or approaches that feel right for you.

SUMMARY

To become authentic teachers, we need first to become aware of those aspects of our Self that are already aspects of being a teacher, then to see how the socially constructed concept of Teacher fits and does not fit with our individual nature. A good place to start sorting these things out is by telling our own story. What was the perspective on teaching in our community and family? How did we decide to become teachers? How have we changed as teachers? This story provides the building blocks for understanding Self as Teacher.

An analysis of what we do in everyday life reveals the

teacher within—those aspects of our personality, values, beliefs, and actions that are our natural way of being a teacher. Teaching is about relating to others in order to help them learn. Relationships are between people. Once we see the teacher who is within our Self, we can bring her into our relationships with students (see Chapter 6).

However, there are strong social perspectives on who teachers are and what they do. Both within the community of educators and in the larger cultural context, there are many and varied views of the role of teacher. Some of these things we may be, by nature, but others we will not be. The teacher without is the conceptualization of teacher that is outside of our nature. Identifying those characteristics and behaviors is equally as important as understanding the natural teacher within us. Trying to live up to outside expectations of what a teacher should be like makes us feel like imposters and frauds.

In order to merge Self and Teacher, we need to differentiate ourselves from the collective or cultural view of teacher. We need to know how we are different from that view and how we are similar. We need to find our unique identity as a teacher and feel strong and certain enough about that identity to bring it into our relationships with students. This is becoming an authentic teacher.

CHAPTER 5

Teacher-Self in Profile

In our efforts to find out who we are as teachers, the theoretical literature is sometimes of little help. It is in the theoretical literature that the social construct of *teacher* is portrayed and often prescribed. What we need to do is to separate ourselves from that construct, finding those parts that fit and those that do not. In Chapter 4, I suggested that telling our own story is a good step in discovering the authentic teacher within ourselves. Listening to the stories of other authentic teachers may be equally helpful. Kohl (1994), among others, argues that teachers' autobiographical stories form a body of knowledge with the potential to help us understand, interpret, and analyze our own experiences in the light of theory.

Brookfield (1995) points out that teachers are skeptical about educational literature because it is written by university academics studying teaching and learning as a discipline. The tone is formal and objective. Practicing teachers feel distant from this formal style and unconnected to writers who have no part in their teaching discipline. "There is none of the hesitation, stumbling, or backtracking that characterize how teachers think about problems of practice" (Brookfield, 1995, p. 38). In a powerful analysis of what he sees as a crisis in teaching, Kincheloe (1991) argues that teachers are "studied down" by educational researchers, and we must negate the cult of the expert through teachers' involvement in understanding their own practice.

Recent literature that incorporates the authentic voices of teachers attempts to bridge the communication gap between educationists and practicing teachers (for example, see Henry,

Huntley, McKamey, & Harper, 1995). We need to hear each other's stories.

In this chapter, I present narratives from four higher education teachers. I had two sources for these stories: I asked colleagues whom I knew, through many conversations with them, to be authentic teachers, and I posted a request for participation on the Professional and Organizational Development (POD) network. From the people who were interested in telling their stories, I selected those who would provide perspectives from a variety of disciplines. The narratives are in the words of the teachers.

KIRSTEN GRAHAM

Helena College of Technology
of The University of Montana

I am never too busy to talk about teaching. I would like to say up front that my teaching style has changed over the years. I has evolved in, I hope, positive directions as I have grown and matured just as we expect our students to grow and mature in our classes. I reserve the right to change, too.

Our teaching environment is pseudo-vocational, pseudo-academic. We are a former vo-tech school now associated with a traditional university and renamed a college of technology. Our mission has expanded so that we now look somewhat occupational but with an academic component. The students in our computer technology curriculum average just under 30 years of age. We run quite a gamut of students, from those with low-level skills and low self-confidence and esteem to those who come to school and suddenly have found themselves. My own unscientific study shows they may have had a tough time in their earlier school experiences and are extremely anxious upon reentering the schoolhouse doors. They wonder if they can "cut the mustard," if they can learn again. My students typically have two—maybe even three—significant jobs; they are full-

time students, full-time parents, and full-time workers. They
come to us in hopes their tough decision was the right one for
them and their families. They have a lot on the line. Many absolutely flourish and their eager learning knows no bounds. In
those cases, I'm the constraint!

My constant underlying thoughts are that I am an autonomous person who values choices and personal responsibility.
And I figure that if I am accustomed to making decisions as an
adult, then our students also have been making major decisions
as a part of being adults, parents, and workers. So who am I to
put them in a dependent classroom situation and remove their
decision making? In addition, as I do some self-reflection, I realize that having choices and making decisions as to which
choice to pursue is important to me. I couple that idea with the
realization that people take our classes for vastly varying reasons. So if I can structure the courses to provide our learners
choices so they can meet their personal goals, then we'll have a
happier, more involved learner. And lastly is the concept of personal responsibility. With choices and decisions come consequences. It is my aim that student choices have valuable, con-
structive consequences, but sometimes the results are less than
pleasing. Personal responsibility wraps up all these ideas. Students keep their own grades—I call them points—and submit a
portfolio of their work at the end of the semester representing
their documentation of the grade they have earned.

I have to remember to balance my personal concepts for
"the way things should be" with offering choices to our students. Sometimes I get carried away with what I think is the
"right way" to do something. I have to realize what I have done
and back away from my good intentions to offering options for
the students. I'm getting better at that the more I practice.

I know our students have their own opinions and I am
(now) OK with hearing their opinions which may differ from
mine. I ask them whether a certain task is helpful or what they
would do to make it better next time. I ask whether they would
recommend a certain exercise to a following student or whether
they would do it again for their own learning.

But again, on the other side of this delicate balance beam, is the nagging reminder that our students come to us for our work history and the knowledge we bring to the classroom. They expect us to guide them in a meaningful, helpful direction that prepares them for the world of work. So as I try to share power and make the classroom more collaborative, something I'm told I do very well, I also have to insure they are getting the very essence of becoming an IT (information technology) worker. For most of our students, this is a transformative experience. They are definitely changed when they leave our doors. We take pride in offering a supportive, nurturing environment, hoping not to become too protective. We do want them to leave! But we take great pride in their successes and accomplishments. That's our job, as I see it.

Teaching has never been a power and control game with me. In my first years of teaching, I felt anything but powerful. But now that I have many years experience under my belt, I am so much more aware of the issue of power, and see being "the teacher" as truly a power position.

But I think it also goes along with expectations. Today's college students are a product of their own K–12 experiences, and those experiences generally are that the teacher is the authority, as are the book and curriculum. I find myself trying pretty hard to undo their expectations of "the typical teacher" and how I am to behave in the classroom. The reason I work at removing the cloak of power is to put the responsibility for their learning squarely on their shoulders. I want them to read critically and to ask questions. I want to empower them to take charge of their learning for a variety of reasons. I guess the number one reason is for them to learn how to learn so that when the training wheels of our school environment are removed, they can continue successfully on without dependency on me or academic structure.

My intent is to challenge students by setting tough standards and then helping them to achieve the high goals. I try to organize my courses so that the learners know up front what is expected of them. I offer them a list of tasks to complete for points. They may work individually or in small groups. Tasks to be accomplished are offered with the proviso they may always propose their own tasks that may better suit their purpose for taking the class. It took me several years to realize people take courses for differing reasons, and that my reasons do not necessarily fit every person!

I believe strongly in the wise words of Malcolm Knowles; "When I stopped controlling I started teaching." So many of my colleagues conspire to give quizzes on Fridays to keep students in their classes. I realized, after a few humbling experiences, that students will attend classes they feel are important and relevant to what they want. When I first started being more open and honest and not being sneaky with Friday quizzes, some attendance took a nosedive. I soon realized that the absences were because I was not teaching material they thought was useful. I revised my approach and the students returned. I have not yet since had attendance "problems" as my colleagues continue to experience.

I want to help students become self-directed learners in preparation for their world of work and the rest of their lives. I would like to infuse them with my own joy and enthusiasm for learning, and I do that by my example and by providing opportunities for those who want to take advantage of them.

I love my job. I love our students and have a great deal of respect for them. True, some try my patience though I find that less so nowadays. I enjoy turning their expectations of what a teacher is upside down and inside out, keeping them on their toes. I think I want them just a little assertive about what they want, and to put demands on me to use their time wisely.

PETER LANE

Maritime Forest Ranger School

Helping people realize how the world works and our place in it is the essence of my teaching. People seem to have an innate desire to move up from wherever they are, to increase their awareness, to discover, to grow. Each person moves in different directions (not always linear), at different speeds (not always constant) and for different reasons (not always clear). It is my privilege to merge or mesh with them wherever they are and help them get to wherever they wish to go.

I can't really say why I'm a teacher. It just feels right to me, and, I would like to add, to my students. Both my parents were teachers so I have always been exposed to the concept and reality of people wanting and needing to learn and the people who want or need to help them. After high school, I attended university intent on becoming a teacher. However, academic life lacked a certain authenticity and connection with my life so I left after the first year. I pumped gas, cut lawns, worked construction, hauled furniture, had a few years on drilling rigs, and a couple more stringing wire for transmission lines up north. Then I had the chance to work with some millwrights on a large hydro-electric project. I was impressed by what they did. They could design and build, modify and improve, and operate and maintain all types of equipment. They worked on complete systems rather than just one part. They needed to be aware of everything in that system, inside and out, top to bottom. This appealed to me.

The one year millwright course at trade school flew by, and I had a great time. Several high school teachers had a positive impact on my life, but it was my trade school instructor who helped me realize some of the things I hold most dear today: the value of earning a living with your hands, of using your head, of negotiating theory with reality, of group cooperation, and of individual determination.

I went to work in the forestry industry, sawmilling to be more exact. Over the years, I acquired experience and knowledge and perhaps more importantly, confidence. I attended another trade school where I specialized in saw design and maintenance and discovered that it was both demanding and satisfying work. Sawmills have a relatively high employee turnover rate so there was plenty of opportunity to watch and help new employees learn. At the time my idealism was not yet tempered by reality; I believed anyone could be taught to do anything. This belief has changed somewhat. I now believe anyone can be taught to do something. I moved around a bit in the Maritime provinces gathering skills and cultural awareness, even living for a while in the United States. Then, my saw maintenance instructor, who was retiring, and who had been tracking my career over the years, called to see if I might be interested in a teaching position.

I knew I had the technical knowledge but would students be willing to listen? Would they want to know what I knew? My instructor convinced me they would, so I put in my notice at my current job and a month later set off to do a job, that, for the first time in my life, wouldn't primarily require the use of my hands. This was no small or easy step, let me tell you. When you work with your hands, you see the results, and you present the calluses as badges of stamina and courage. (The spots we sometimes rub raw while teaching don't show as easily and they certainly aren't displayed proudly. I sometimes wonder why that is.)

I returned to university part-time—on a mission this time. My predecessor warned me that a university education should never get in the way of actually learning something useful. Now, being a couple of courses away from my education degree, I can say with some regret that I understand what he meant. But, for the most part university has been good to me. I selected courses I felt pertinent—lesson planning, public speaking, personality types, group dynamics, and the like, and they have helped me more fully understand the process of teaching and learning.

So here I am, teaching several courses and administering several more at a training institution designed to provide practical training to the forestry industry. Students who are sent by their companies are exposed to a mixture of classroom activities, hands-on experiences, and field trips to industry. I have come to know many different instructors, and I have noticed that some are more effective than others. The difference, I believe, lies in establishing connection to reality—not the instructor's reality nor the institution's but that of the students. An instructor who takes the time to connect to students helps them move further along their desired path.

In my own courses, the first day is spent gathering specifications on the machines the participants use on the job. Students call, fax, or e-mail their machine designer, builder, installer, and parts supplier. They begin to realize the training will be about them and their needs. This is a powerful motivator. Then we learn some concepts and principles. Next, we apply the specs and concepts to the school's equipment and see how it performs. Now it's time to visit some manufacturing plants. In all the years we have requested tours, we have never been refused; I believe this indicates good things about our work. Next we go back to the school to put it all together in order to solve the students' individual problems. Finally, a clear list of things to do when they arrive back on the job is generated with and for each student.

For me authentic teaching and learning is about the acquisition and application of knowledge and skills. It involves a balance of many components: big picture and small details, technical aspects and human feelings, logical and intuitive processes, traditional and experimental teaching, the employee and the company, calm times and confusion. Authenticity is not a method. It is a mindset. It is a genuine desire to progress, to improve, to grow and to be more. It is a willingness to suspend belief in the face of what is. When I have a particularly good class I'll schedule an extra three-hour night session. This results in extra commitment from students, a tighter group bond, higher retention, and even better manual skills. It's as if the higher-thinking mind is put on hold while a deeper connection is realized between the students and their work. Perhaps this is some kind of throwback to our ancestors when we had to huddle around the campfire at night for protection from the elements. I don't know the reason nor do I really need to. It is simply one thing which brings it all home to students in a more meaningful way. The class often ends up being four hours instead of three.

Learning certainly isn't a straight line leading up. We often revisit our favorite places. When I think about the fact that I'll graduate from university more than twenty-five years after I started bothers me. However, when I reflect on my life and values, and I realize that everything has progressed quite naturally for me, you might even say, quite authentically, I feel a whole lot better about who I am and what I do.

SUSAN B. WESLEY

University of Maine & Arcadia Hospital

Being an authentic teacher, to me, is built upon two essential aspects of character. The first is an unquenchable thirst for self-awareness. The second is passion for one's discipline. Harry Chapin's "All My Life's a Circle" almost fits, but I prefer the symbol of a spiral, as I have pursued authenticity in my teaching with a focus on growing self-awareness and tending the fire for my passion for music.

The old saying, "the more things change, the more they stay the same," seems to describe my lifelong involvement in teaching. From my early years of teaching the kids next door how to play hop scotch to teaching Sunday school in my teen years, to the beginning of my formal teaching career over 32 years ago, it could be said that I have been teaching a very long time. Music was my earliest passion and merged with my excitement to take the experience of music to everyone through teaching and became my profession even before graduating with a BMEd. in 1970.

My passion for music and the excitement of faces in the classroom or rehearsal when "they got it" was contagious for me. But I didn't understand that at first. I *did* teach early in my life, but I didn't call it teaching, nor did I honor the patience and persistence I brought to it. So when in my late teens I discovered that the essence of the discipline which I loved so dearly was my ticket to a career, one might say I discovered my profession — Music Education!

The years have not changed my desire to work within the discipline of music, but the years have enriched the spectrum where I find my work today. Over time, I have been unraveling, for myself, learning about the power of music in my life. Working with hospice patients, children, and adults with severe handicapping conditions, emotionally and psychologically battered and traumatized populations, and doing my own personal analytical psychological work, I am increasingly in awe of how much more there is to human experience in learning as well as what can enhance and block learning.

It was striking to me that so many adults could be music phobic when invited to participate in songs or playing even the most harmless of instruments such as a tambourine. It didn't take long to discover that most of the fear I ran into came from adults whose aesthetic senses were developmentally delayed, so to speak. Such delays were often due to inappropriate teacher comments and language they experienced in their childhood. I became committed to becoming as self-aware as I could so that I wouldn't injure any of my students the way I found so many adults to have been injured. This insight and commitment was made in my fourth year of teaching and I've been in hot pursuit of enlightenment since.

Enlightenment comes to me if I am present with my students, clients, and patients. The quality of presence is my strong suit. I really love the brainstorming, what-if, many-possibilities approach to life. But in service to my varied populations, I must be present and, at the same time, keep the possibilities approach sitting close at hand for other ways of meeting what the individual or group might present. My values are firmly held around the goals of investigation and integration in service to individuation. I work with my students, clients, and patients from a model of andragogy. Even with my youngest charges, I provide structure within which they might explore and identify their freedoms and label their boundaries.

Now I should explain that within my teaching career, spanning preschool through graduate school and Elderhostel, I have also maintained a private practice in psychotherapy and music. I work from a Jungian orientation in my private practice and case load at a local psychiatric hospital. But I must admit that my overall orientation even in the classroom is also quite

Jungian. From such an orientation, I have examined my teaching practices (both subjectively and through my students giving me anonymous feedback weekly) and find that I often work with aspects of my character which I do not consciously know are operating at times but that are, indeed, observed by my students. Likewise, I do choose, from time to time, to use exercises and activities such as targeted readings, thematic video clips and other media assignments that might "push buttons." It feels like instigating to me, but such activities can ignite unkindled potential and interest.

I have taught directly in the discipline of music and the field of music education for more than 32 years, and I have also worked in the field of adult education for 28 years. The field of psychotherapy has been part-time for me since 1988, but I am now working full-time in private practice and part-time in teaching (in the formal sense). The fundamental underpinnings of my authenticity, I believe, are aesthetic awareness and development in service to the Self, mine, as well as the student, client, and patient.

LAURENCE ROBERT COHEN

Independent Educator, Tuscon, Arizona

Expressing myself about my authenticity as a teacher may somehow imply a kind of singular achievement, a state of being that I have come to at some point. Authenticity and my Self form a permanent and near perfected unity. I am authentic. I be this authenticity. But authenticity doesn't be in that sense at all. We can try to see the authentic as this thing, a trophy we can capture if we follow the right rules and structures. Then we have it. We can hang it on the wall with our other degrees and awards: "Laurence Robert Cohen, Authentic Teacher, Lifetime Certificate." It doesn't come that way. It makes more demands than that. I and we have the responsibility to choose how we define the living thing of authenticity.

In the Bible, Moses asks God for a name to tell his people. In one translation, God responds, "I am that I am." In another translation, God answers, "I am that I am becoming." In my unity with authenticity, I choose the second translation. My authenticity doesn't be, it becomes. It exists as a constant force of change and growth. At times, authenticity and I don't feel like a unity but an opposition as it makes demands for reflection and action that drag my Self once more out of some comfortable self I have settled into. Authenticity doesn't come as a desire to settle and farm. It comes as a desire for search and discovery. The impulse to authenticity means that the face of authenticity changes in a never ending process endlessly abandoning previous states of true and valuable authenticity to discover present potentiality made possible by the past attainment. Authenticity becomes itself but never completely fulfills itself or my Self.

Authenticity and my Self form a unity, and we are also legion. Acting out of authenticity, I involve countless incarnations of my Self over time in my teaching, into all learning encounters, and I draw from any and all of them as the moment demands. Out of the my past comes a Self of fifteen who hated school and teachers and regimentation. That Self knew a face of education that my current Self dare not forget. That fifteen-year-old will always knows the sting of powerlessness, devaluation, and degradation that comes in the commanding and dominating presence of inauthentic teachers. Those teachers always know and command what happens in their classrooms. Any deviation from their unequivocal knowing of systematic and unchanging truth is wrong, guilty and punishable accordingly. That fifteen-year-old part of me forms part of the inner voice of authenticity and forever questions and goads about my practice. It always wants to know if I have slipped into the teacher-as-demigod-of-truth thereby making my students some form of worshipers or sacrifices at my altar. This voice and command of authenticity also demands to know how everyone in my learning encounters shares power, so they can value and grade themselves.

In this past semester this manifestation of authenticity led me to shift evaluation and grading over to my students with stunningly fine results. My rediscovery of the learning encounter comes from many places and much study, but it will also always come from the 15-year-old who hated school and left it behind for 20 years. He forms part of the I and we of my authentic Self.

Other voices form part of the legion of authenticity and myself. My authenticity demands I listen and consider other voices, student voices, as valid as my own. I found an authentic moment during an administrative fuss about how to officially identify "learning disabled students," an inauthentic epithet if I ever heard one, so they could have more time during exams. I tried to cut through all that official identification and told my students that if they would simply self-identify as, what I called, "learning different," they could have whatever time they needed. I admit to feeling quite pleased about that solution which may well have been inauthentic in itself. A student asked why she had to identify herself as anything in order to get more time. Why couldn't she just have it? I answered that I didn't know. It was a good question. It was the question. So I thought about it. After some thinking out loud, I answered that I had no idea why she couldn't, so she could, and so could anyone else. That voice and that moment form part of the process of my authenticity.

My authentic teaching asks for my students' authentic involvement. They come to the subject and the learning encounter as whole people with complete lives. That demands that I arrive in the same spirit, in the same wholeness. It means that my present life also come to class when it fits. Out of authenticity, I self-disclose. My love for my family, Silvia and Gavin, come to every learning encounter with me because they have such a central part in my life, and I learn so much from them. When the moment requires that sort of involvement, my family come to teach with me.

Authenticity calls for us, as Viktor Frankl might say, to search for the meaning in the moment. In any learning encounter, we want to find that meaning and share that meaning with each other. Each of these moments leads to other such moments because meaning remains in the process of becoming as authentic learning encounters remain in that process. This seeking and finding and making meaning does not imply agreement with a single result, a single immutable truth. It does imply that those who form part of this authentic encounter accept that we have engaged in a meaningful act with a meaningful result even if we do not always agree on the manifestation of that meaning. In working at becoming my authentic Self, I must call on those with whom I engage in learning to become their authentic Selves, not to be an extension of my self through constant agreement. If my authenticity has autonomy and integrity, as it must, their authenticity must have autonomy and integrity as well.

SUMMARY

In these and the many other stories I received from teachers who see themselves as authentic, I searched for commonalities or themes. I see three major themes, which together form a circle, cycle, or spiral describing authenticity.

First, it seems that not only did all of these teachers know themselves well, but also that they had come to differentiate themselves from the collective of the teaching community—to know how they differ and to express these differences with confidence. Laurence Robert Cohen speaks of "cutting through" the official policy on identifying learning disabled students; Kirsten Graham rejects the Friday quizzes her colleagues use to ensure attendance. As a part of their self-awareness, these teachers know from whence they have come. Although their journeys vary, they know the path they have traveled and feel they have ended up in the right place. Peter Lane left university the first time when it was not relevant to his life, but returned years later "on a mission," and now sees his progression into teaching as quite natural. Susan Wesley described a lifelong involvement in teaching and an incremental process of enrichment through her experience. I see in each of these stories a theme of individuation. Each teacher established and continues to establish his or her personal identity as a teacher.

Second, individuation seems to lead to a sense of empowerment for all teachers. The teachers feel empowered themselves as a product of having a solid sense of who they are, and they also shift that concept over to their students. Kirsten asks, "So who am I to put them in a dependent classroom situation and remove their decision making?" Peter speaks of helping students get to wherever *they* want to go. Susan works to help students overcome the constraint of music phobia and describes how she provides a structure within which her students "explore and identify their freedoms and label their boundaries." Laurence shifts the power intrinsic in the evaluation and grading process over to his students "with stunningly fine results," and links this decision directly to his own 15-year old Self who hated school.

Third, I see this sense of empowerment, both within the teacher and within her or his students, leading to authenticity. The teacher who has established individuality, feels empowered as a result of doing so, and thereby sets out to empower students, also genuinely expresses these views to her students and others within the professional community. Kirsten works hard to undo students' expectations about the typical teacher and speaks out directly to her students about who she is as a teacher. Peter doesn't hesitate to schedule an additional three-hour night session for his students to keep up the momentum of a particularly good class. Susan writes about the quality of her presence and working with aspects of her character which she may not even be conscious of at any one time. Laurence says, "I don't know" when a student asks why she couldn't "just have" more time during an exam, then realizes if he has no idea why she couldn't, she could.

The example from Laurence's story showed how authenticity leads back to individuation, closing the circle. He genuinely did not know why students could not have the time they needed, without identifying themselves as learning disabled or "learning different." He expressed this. Through the expression, he realized he must act in a way that was congruent with the question having no answer. In doing so, he further differentiated himself from the teaching collective in which it is assumed, without question, that exams have a time limit.

In this chapter four authentic teachers told us how they see themselves, how they are distinct from the social construct of *teacher*, how they are empowered by their personal perspective on teaching, how they work to empower their students, how they express themselves authentically to their students and others, and how this expression leads them to further clarity as to who they are as teachers and human beings.

CHAPTER 6

Connecting with Students

Teaching is a special sort of communication between people with the goal of fostering learning. In order to communicate in a meaningful way, there must be some connection between the people involved in the communication. At the very least, one person speaks to another with some awareness of the person to whom he is speaking, and another person listens with some awareness of the person to whom she is listening. The greater the connection, or relationship, between the people, the more likely the communication is meaningful. If one or both people are unauthentic, playing roles or wearing masks, the relationship rests on a false foundation. We then relate to the mask, and the mask is not the person. Teaching, I suggest, is based on a relationship between people who are being authentic.

Being authentic does not mean revealing all, expressing feelings, or spending a great deal of time together. The relationship between teacher and student need not involve self-disclosure; in fact, self-disclosure could be inauthentic if a person is not inclined, by nature, to engage in self-disclosure, or if self-disclosure is self-serving and has little or no connection to learning. Being authentic in relationships with students means, simply, being yourself during communications with students.

To understand another person—to relate to her—we work at at least two levels. Intellectually, we may understand a person's experience, culture, beliefs, and preferences. As teachers, we know students come from a variety of backgrounds and have different learning styles and personalities. On an affective level, we feel. Writing more than two decades ago, Curran's (1978) words capture this better than any I have seen since.

Even though the person may be teaching as a knower, he, in turn, is deeply in need sometimes of being understood in his affective state, since his whole personal status is invested in what he is saying. The reverse can also be true. The student may be profoundly committed in a personal status to the question he has asked or to the point of view he is presenting. Therefore, while his language appears to be the language of cognition, it can be highly packaged in the language of affect. Now, the knower-teacher becomes the understander, sensitively helping the student, the learner, to separate these two until the clarity of a cognition emerges so that he can see and say, "Now I see and that fits." (pp. 5–6)

To connect with our students, to enter into an authentic relationship with them in order to communicate and teach, requires self-understanding. As Hollis (1998, p. 13) says, *"the quality of all our relationships is a direct function of our relationship to ourselves,"* and *"the best thing we can do for our relationships with others, and with the transcendent, then, is to render our relationship to ourselves more conscious"* [italics in the original].

Teachers and students bring their Self to the relationship. As I discuss in Chapter 4, teachers are differentiated from the social construct of teacher to varying degrees; similarly students may be differentiated, or not, from the social construct of student. Both teacher and student are individuals with a unique and complex set of characteristics. Both teacher and student are a part of the collective of the teaching and learning community, the larger collective of their culture, and the global collective of humanity.

In this chapter, I describe three kinds of connections we have with students. Although there are as many different relationships as there are students, I believe that looking for patterns within the ways we communicate with students can be helpful in working toward authenticity. I portray the protégé, the student with whom we identify, the critic, the student who challenges us, and the enemy, the student with whom we cannot relate. In the fourth part of the chapter, I discuss how we connect with groups and how groups develop an identity which is more than that of a collection of individuals.

THE PROTÉGÉ

As Kuhlenschmidt (1999) points out, our emotional reactions to events and people have an internal source—they come from within. Two instructors may react in quite different ways to the same student, depending on their nature, past experiences, and assumptions about good students. When we meet a protégé, something clicks. We identify with the person, see her as like ourselves, and easily fall into the role of becoming a model or mentor. Hollis (1998) sees projection as being at the center of our search for the magical other, the person with whom we can have a relationship. Projection occurs unconsciously when we attribute our own traits, values, and flaws to another. As soon as we become aware of projection—make it conscious—we are already in the process of taking it back. When projection fails, it is usually because the other person has failed to catch, hold, and reflect our projection.

When we see a student as a protégé, it is something within us that leads us to this interpretation of that student. It is something to do with how we see ourselves. If we accept the Jungian language, we unconsciously project our own qualities on the student, and if the projection fits, if the student reflects how we see ourselves, the connection is established. If we prefer not to talk about relationships with students in terms of projection, we can also describe this process as simply one of being drawn to or interested in people with whom we feel an affinity, with whom we share common interests, abilities, and attitudes.

When we have the opportunity, we may enter into a mentoring relationship with a student whom we see as a protégé. In the adult education literature, a fair bit of attention has been paid to the role of mentors (for example, see a classic book on mentoring by Daloz, 1986, or Cohen, 1995), though it is too often described as a unidirectional process in which a more experienced person provides guidance to a novice. I use the term here to describe a relationship that is more collaborative in nature. Sgroi and Saltiel (1998) list the key elements in collaborative human connections as including deep trust and respect, a

shared goal or purpose, complementary but different tempera-
ments, synergy, and mutual, free choice of the other. Hiemstra
and Brockett (1998) provide a good personal example of such a
relationship.

We all love to encounter students whom we see as protégés.
This is where we feel we can contribute to meaningful changes
in others' lives; this is what teaching should be all about. Sometimes, with large classes and busy schedules, it is frustrating not
to be able to spend the individual time we would like with a
protégé, but usually this is the student we make time for. It is
relatively easy to be an authentic teacher when working with a
protégé. We see ourselves in the student, he sees himself in us,
and there are few roles to play. One danger may be that we become a bit too puffed up with our own importance as the student looks up to us as a wise advisor. Another danger can be
overstepping the boundary between teacher and student and en-
tering into an inappropriate or personal relationship that inter-
feres with teaching and learning.

In Exercise 6.1, I suggest an activity to encourage reflection
on our relationships with students whom we have seen as pro-
teges. In order to understand how we connect with students, it
is useful to contemplate specific relationships.

THE CRITIC

"What do you mean by that?" "I can't accept that point of
view." "I think you have made a mistake in logic in that explanation." "Have you considered what Jürgen Habermas says on
this?" "Last night, I was reading a different perspective, derived
from critical social theory, and I would say you could interpret
that in an entirely different way." "I don't see how you could
make this comment on my essay." "As I was saying to the group
before class, I think we could have had a more recent reading
on this topic." "It seems to me we are wasting time with this
discussion." "Why don't you tell us your views rather than have
us work it out in groups?"

We all have encountered the student as critic. We may feel

Exercise 6.1 Who Are Your Protégés?

Reflect on your teaching for the past few years. Which students would you describe as protégés? List some of their names here.

What words or phrases would you use to describe the types of interactions you had with these students (for example, stimulating, challenging, warm, respectful)?

Review your list of names, bringing images of these students into your mind and concentrating on their personalities, learning styles, values, or other characteristics. What do they have in common?

How many of these characteristics do you share with them?

---

uncomfortable and defensive. We may view the student as a troublemaker or a too-dominant class member who needs to be taken aside and "talked to." Our position of power and authority seems to be undermined. Dirkx (1997, p. 80) tells the story of Clara, a student who angrily said, "You know, I am getting so sick of group work in this class!" Dirkx comments, "Rarely do I take such attacks personally, but Clara's behavior and concerns seemed to come from left field, and I experienced strong feelings of betrayal, anger, and defensiveness." He reports that he "quickly moved into information-giving, which lasted the rest of the session" (p. 81) and that the incident left the class limping "along emotionally deflated and anemic for the remainder of the term" (p. 81). In other words, the connection was broken.

A student may be a critic for a variety of reasons. She may be an experienced, well-read, intelligent student whose expertise seems to challenge our own. Or, the critic may be an insecure student, a person who tries to establish his own self-esteem by attacking others, both classmates and teacher. Sometimes a critic is a person who has a nature similar to our own, but with a different twist. In terms of psychological type preferences (see Chapter 1), a student may share one of our preferred functions, but have a different dominant (or auxiliary) function and thereby be critical of that difference. For example, if the teacher has a dominant thinking function and a secondary sensing function, and the student prefers thinking and intuition, she may be impatient with the teacher's emphasis on concrete details. Other times, differences in values or past experiences may provoke the critical student.

How do we maintain authenticity with the student critic? If our confidence in our teaching rests on the power we gain from being in the position of teacher, the critic is a dangerous beast indeed. If we are reflective teachers, open to considering alternatives and willing to question our own assumptions, the student critic can provide a welcome challenge. If we have thought through what we do and why we do it, the critic can give us an opportunity to be explicit about our philosophy of practice. However, it is one thing to intellectually welcome challenges, and it is quite another how we may *feel* under these circumstances. As I quoted from Curran (1978) at the beginning of the chapter, sometimes, as teachers, we are deeply in need of being understood in the affective state. As human beings, we want to be liked, and respected; as teachers we want to be admired as "knowers."

What would have happened had John Dirkx, whose story about Clara I quoted earlier, said authentically to Clara and the class, "I feel angry and defensive," or "I feel stuck, I don't know what to do now?" I suspect the outcome would have been different.

A few years ago, a student had given me an extensive journal and asked me to make comments. I spent several hours with the journal, making long remarks in the margins and asking questions about what he had written. His next journal entry, which he also gave to me, was sharp and abrupt. He resented my comments. I was hurt and angry. I returned his short journal entry with no comments, or perhaps an equally short comment, I cannot recall that now. That evening, my response to him did not sit well with me. I wrote him a rather long note in which I explained my reasons for my comments—I was interested in what he wrote, I felt I had something to say about it. I also told him that I was upset by his sharp reply, and I speculated on why I had this reaction. My note was authentic and it served to reconnect me with the student. He and I still correspond regularly.

Being authentic with the student critic involves being honest, both intellectually and emotionally. If we don't know something and have been challenged on it, we must say we don't know. If we feel hurt or uncertain as to how to respond, we should, in some way that is authentic to our nature, convey that response.

In Exercise 6.2, I recommend that we take a moment to think about who our critics have been and how we have responded to them.

THE ENEMY

We are not supposed to dislike students. That we sometimes do is a secret most of us keep well-hidden except from the closest of friends or disguise through the telling of funny stories about students. Yet, why should we expect, out of the hundreds of students we work with, that we authentically like each of them. We are quite comfortable disliking a neighbor or a colleague, but we feel we must like all students. When the dislike is mutual, we have student as enemy. Perhaps it is even more difficult when we dislike a student who seems to admire or like us.

There are few references to disliking students in the literature. Brookfield (1990), in *The Skillful Teacher*, includes a section in which he advises us not to play favorites: "there are those

---

Exercise 6.2 Who Are Your Critics?

Take a few minutes to think back over students who have been your critics. List some of their names here.

_____   _____   _____

_____   _____   _____

_____   _____   _____

Choose one or two of your student critics and recall how you responded to their challenges. Consider especially whether or not you were true to yourself in your reactions. If you find you were not, write down here what you could have said or done differently.

_____

_____

_____

---

whom you dislike personally, whom you think boorish and insensitive, and whom you believe are sliding through a course with a minimum of effort and a maximum of cynical contempt" (p. 171). He goes on to say firmly, "if you are ever to be trusted by students, it is absolutely essential that you don't allow yourself the luxury of exercising these personal dislikes" (p. 171).

How we work with the enemy may depend on why we see him as an enemy. We may dislike students who are opposite in nature from us. If we are logical and well-organized, we may dislike the student who comes into class late with crumpled papers, which we suspect are his course notes, trailing behind him. If we are warm and caring, we may dislike the student who is cold and arrogant in her discussions with classmates. We tend not to like, or at least have a great deal of difficulty understanding, a person whose psychological type preferences are opposite to ours (see Chapter 1).

We may also dislike students whom we see as disinterested in the class, cynical, bored, or unwilling to participate in learning activities. Such students seem to be making a statement about our own competence as teachers or perhaps making light of a subject area which we obviously care about and believe in. If we work hard to engage students in learning, try to inspire interest, and take extra time with those students who seem uninvolved, the antagonistic or disinterested student is an affront to our efforts.

How does an authentic teacher behave in these situations? Obviously, being open about our feelings is not the answer here. But, does this make us unauthentic? The authentic teacher cares about teaching, believes in its value, wants to work well with students, and has a professional respect for students in general. She reflects on her practice. She tries to understand what she can do better. Not liking a student is bound to happen; the authentic teacher wants to know why and what to do. In other words, professionalism and ethical, moral behavior take over. Kingwell (1995) argues that when we share a public space, we use *tact*, we resist our desire to express ourselves fully. Being a teacher is more than being a person in a social situation. Working in a classroom with a group of people is not the same as being at a barbecue in the neighbor's backyard. At the neighbor's, it is acceptable to avoid lengthy conversations with someone we do not like. In the classroom, it is not.

If the dislike is based on opposing personality characteristics, we can learn something from the student about differences among human beings. The student does not need to become our friend, but we must accept that each way of being in the world is valid, and go about understanding this different way of being. Holding ourselves open to learning about nature that is foreign to our own can be a valuable and rewarding experience.

If our dislike for a student is based on our perception of that person being disinterested or even hostile toward us or the subject area, we need to look beyond the feeling that we have been personally insulted. Perhaps the student is anxious, lacking in confidence, or afraid of making a fool of himself by revealing what he does not know and covering up these fears with aggressive remarks. Perhaps the student is a single parent and works at night to support her family and is exhausted when she is in class. Perhaps we do not make things clear to the student, or relate the subject area to his experiences, and he cannot make head nor tail out of what we are saying. What we need to do is to find out the reasons for the student's resistance and, when possible, work to overcome it. At the same time, we must realize that we cannot be all things to all students, nor can we force someone to learn. There will be occasions when there is nothing we can do.

In Exercise 6.3, I suggest that we reflect on students we have perceived as enemies and how we have behaved with them.

When I completed this exercise, I realized that my own tendency with students whom I dislike has been to hide my reaction through overcompensation. What I have done on some occasions is to *pretend* I am very fond of the student—an unauthentic practice which is unfair to the student and uncomfortable for me.

THE GROUP

Whether we work with classes of ten students or two hundred, a group atmosphere emerges. Especially with smaller groups, there is a "collective spirit" and a "collective truth" that includes a "realization of the power that rests in a group, particularly when it tackles some problem that no individual could deal with alone" (Apps, 1996, pp. 101–102). However, even in large classes, we can usually characterize the group, or perhaps subgroups, in some way. We talk about large classes as being boisterous, serious, noisy, difficult to manage, passive, or enthusiastic. From the students' perspective, large classes can have an anonymous and impersonal nature that leads to inappropriate and disruptive behavior (Carbone, 1999).

Heimlich and Norland (1994, p. 153) point out that individual students are an important part of instruction, but "not necessarily the greatest part." When we teach, we almost always are working not with individual people, nor with a collection of individuals, but with a group. We connect with and relate to individuals in the group, but we also relate to the group as a whole. At the same time, students in a group are relating to each

---

Exercise 6.3 Who Are Your Enemies?

Recall students whom you have disliked. Think of those whom you personally regarded as enemies. Write their names here.

_____ _____ _____

_____ _____ _____

_____ _____ _____

Focus on just one name from your list. Recall how he or she looked, what he or she said, and how you felt at the time of your interactions. Describe the student and your feelings.

_____

_____

_____

Why did you dislike this student? Focus on the one person.

_____

_____

How did you behave with him or her?

_____

_____

Consider whether or not her or his behavior could have been related to something outside of the classroom, or whether your dislike was based on personality. If, in retrospect, there is anything you would like to have done differently, describe it here.

_____

_____

_____

---

other in a variety of ways, and, as teachers, we are group members.

How do we relate authentically to the group? To some extent, as I write elsewhere (Cranton, 1996), our relationship with a group depends on the nature of the learning the group is engaged in. We may be the person who designs exercises, activities, and problems; we may be an equal participant in shared inquiry;

or, we may be the one to stimulate critical self-reflection and questioning. But, regardless of the various ways we facilitate different kinds of learning, we need to be an authentic voice in the group.

In their discussion of "dispositions" that foster democratic discussion in a group, Brookfield and Preskill (1999) list ten ideals: hospitality, participation, mindfulness, humility, mutuality, deliberation, appreciation, hope, and autonomy. For the teacher interested in authentic relations with the student group, several of these are especially relevant. We not only need to create a hospitable environment which is receptive to new ideas and perspectives, but we also need to do ourselves everything we ask students to do. Mindfulness involves being fully aware of what is being said and by whom, of truly connecting with what students say. Humility is being open to admitting the boundaries and limitations of our knowledge and expertise, and being willing to learn from our students. With mutuality, we allow the line between teacher and student to become blurred as the whole group, including the teacher, takes responsibility for teaching and learning. Openly expressing appreciation to the student group builds trust and a sense of community.

As authentic teachers, we contribute to the development and growth of the group by sharing our knowledge, resources, expertise, and our person. We challenge, support, guide, and come into conflict with the collective spirit and collective truth of the group.

SUMMARY

Jarvis (1992, p. 113) writes, "Authentic action is to be found when individuals freely act in such a way that they try to foster the growth and development of each other's being." The authentic actions of teachers lead them to learn and grow together with their students. "Instructors who merely expound their knowledge in an authoritative manner are in no position to learn from their students" (pp. 114–115). Being authentic as a teacher fosters good and meaningful relationships with students.

In this chapter, I reviewed three prototypes of students with whom we relate. I am not suggesting they are representative of all relationships with students, but rather I presented them as important and perhaps challenging connections. The protégé is the student upon whom we pin our hopes for the future, and also, often, the student whom we see as like ourselves. The critic is the student who challenges our knowledge or our teaching competence or both. The enemy is the student whom, sometimes inexplicably, we dislike and to whom we feel we cannot relate. We need to remain authentic and professional in each of these relationships.

Given the complexity of relationships among people, it should not be surprising that each teacher sees different characteristics in the same student. Your protégé will not be mine. The student I see as a critic you may not even notice. And my enemy will not be yours. The way we connect with our students is based on who we are. Hollis (1998) proposes four principles of relationship: what we do not know or want to accept about ourselves, we project onto others; we project our wounds and longings onto others; when the other person refuses responsibility for our wounds and longings, projection gives away to resentment and issues of power; and, the only way to heal a faltering relationship is to take personal responsibility for our own individuation. In other words, the quality of our relationships with students depends on how well we know ourselves and how authentically we bring ourselves to the relationship.

In the final part of the chapter, I discussed how the authentic teacher relates to the group. "All life is relational," Hollis (1998, p. 101) writes. Sociologists distinguish between a society and a community. As opposed to a society, where people are organized to serve a certain purpose, a community forms whenever people have a common experience that lifts each person out of his or her isolation to participate in the transformation. The authentic teacher can help the classroom to become a vital community by giving of her Self to the group.

CHAPTER 7

Teacher-Self in Context

Teaching is a social process that takes place in a context. In spite of the ivory tower metaphor that comes to many people's minds when they think of college and university teaching, the essence of teaching is social and political change, and good teaching is a democratic process. The image of the helpless, absent-minded professor who could not function in the real world and has taken refuge in teaching is obsolete. Yet, we rarely find the context of teaching addressed in the literature.

Nesbit (1998) points out that discussions of teaching downplay the influence of subject-matter and situational, political, and social contexts. In his empirical study of adult educators, he found teachers driven by the curriculum and the context within which they worked. Nesbit refers to Cuban's (1993) notion of situationally constrained choice as an explanation for the teacher's behavior. Teachers have some autonomy, but their actions are influenced by external factors, by context.

Most of the writing about teaching and learning focuses on an individualistic conception of the person, ignoring the person in society or in state. Jarvis (1992) sees teaching as an ethical problem. "Learning is about becoming a person in society," he writes, "but paradoxically, learning is also about adapting and becoming a conforming member of society" (p. 237). Teaching assists in both endeavors. Teachers mediate between the sociocultural world and the student; to a certain extent, they interpret that world for students. Teachers have taken over the role previously performed by priests or elders in the community—the role of passing on cultural knowledge. The importance of recognizing the influence of context on our work cannot be over-looked in our search for authenticity.

In this chapter, I examine four levels of the teaching context. The structure or type of knowledge in our discipline can either enhance or hinder authentic teaching. Similarly, the nature of the institution within which we work can encourage or squelch authenticity. A variety of communities, groups we identify with, influence how we perceive ourselves as teachers. Finally, within the broader state and society is a perspective or worldview on teachers' work that informs many of our beliefs and assumptions about what we do.

THE DISCIPLINE

Teaching mathematics is different from teaching social work even when we take our authentic self into the context. Teaching introductory psychology is different from teaching a graduate seminar in cognitive psychology. The discipline within which we work and the level at which we teach it provide a certain structure. When that structure matches our basic nature, values, and preferences, we hardly notice it, except perhaps to wonder why some students cannot see things as clearly as we can. However, sometimes the discipline does not coincide with the way we think or feel, and this can lead to a struggle to be authentic in fostering learning in that discipline.

There are many ways to classify knowledge. Philosophers recognize three main kinds of knowledge: factual knowledge or *knowledge that*, practical knowledge or *knowledge how*, and knowledge of people, places, and things, or *knowledge by acquaintance* (Vesey & Foulkes, 1990). Cognitive psychologists such as Anderson (1983) distinguish between declarative and procedural knowledge, declarative knowledge being what we know about things (facts) and procedural knowledge being our knowledge about how to perform various skills and tasks. Psychologists are also interested in expert and novice knowledge, deep and surface knowledge, and other systems which reveal the progression involved in the acquisition of knowledge. Educators have worked to develop ways of classifying knowledge that can be used in planning instruction. Hauenstein (1998), for example, reminds us that individuals learn as a whole person, using their senses to receive information, intellect to process it, muscles to perform actions, and feelings to react to the experience. Accordingly, he classifies knowledge as cognitive, affective, psychomotor, and behavioral, the latter domain being an integration of the previous three in which knowledge is acted upon.

Elsewhere, I have relied on Habermas's (1971) description of kinds of knowledge and have found this to be a useful framework (for example, see Cranton, 1998b). Until recently, Habermas was with the Frankfurt School of critical theory. His classification system has been widely applied in education (Ewert, 1991); his work is used internationally in philosophy, political science, and sociology.

Habermas identifies three kinds of knowledge. *Instrumental knowledge* allows us to manipulate and control the environment, predict observable physical and social events, and take appropriate actions. Empirical or scientific methodologies produce this technically useful knowledge. Knowledge is established by reference to external reality; there is an objective world made up of observable phenomena. The laws governing physical and social systems can be identified through science and are seen to operate independently of human perceptions. Many disciplines rely on instrumental knowledge, including trades and technologies such as marine or automobile mechanics, silviculture, dental hygiene, and computer electronics. Studies in the health professions contain a good proportion of instrumental knowledge. Curriculum in the sciences, such as biology, chemistry, physics, and geological sciences are derived directly from the empirical-analytical approach.

Communicative knowledge is our understanding, based on language, of each other and the social norms which influence us. We live together in groups, communities, cultures, and nations in order to satisfy our mutual needs and interests. Within a society, we have a code of commonly accepted beliefs and behaviors. We come to agree on how things are or should be in reference to standards and values, moral and political issues, educational and social systems, and government actions. Communicative knowledge is acquired through shared interpretation and consensus. Disciplines such as psychology, sociology, politics, education, language, literature, fine arts, and history deal primarily with communicative knowledge—human behavior is studied on an individual or social scale. Applied programs, including child studies, early childhood education, special education, social work, nursing, occupational therapy, and hospitality involve acquiring knowledge about how to work with others.

Emancipatory knowledge is self-knowledge leading to growth, development, and freedom from oppression. Gaining emancipatory knowledge is dependent on our ability to be self-determining and self-reflective—aware and critical of ourselves and of our social and cultural context. The philosophical foundation of emancipatory knowledge lies in critical theory. Instrumental and communicative knowledge are not rejected, but are seen as limiting. If we do not question current scientific and social theories, we may never realize how we are constrained by them. Emancipatory knowledge is relevant to all disciplines, especially at the higher levels of study.

Teachers with different psychological type preferences, values, and experiences may embrace one kind of knowledge over others. Those who have a dominant thinking or sensing function (see Chapter 1), for example, would work well in disciplines which are founded on instrumental knowledge. Teachers who are more intuitive in nature may be drawn to the emancipatory domain, and those with a strong feeling function may be naturally attracted to fields where communicative knowledge is emphasized. Similarly, our experience and background, especially the kind of knowledge that has been valued in the communities or institutions where we work, may influence our comfort level with one discipline over another.

To be authentic teachers, to be true to ourselves in our work, it is important to be aware of how our natures fit with the predominant kind of knowledge in our discipline. This is not to say that only thinking types should teach mathematics or computer technology, or only feeling types should teach coun-

seling. In fact, people working in disciplines that are not completely congruent with their natures can bring new perspectives
into the discipline, work better with a variety of students, and
challenge the status quo. But, it can be a struggle, too, especially
if we do not understand why teaching certain things is difficult
or just does not sit right with us. Most often, we are drawn to
disciplines that suit our nature, and the research confirms this
(for example, see Myers, 1995). However, for a variety of reasons such as family expectations, lack of knowledge about options, accessibility of higher education, or financial constraints,
people find themselves working in fields they may not have chosen otherwise. It is good to know this and to develop ways of
teaching that are authentic within the context of the discipline.

As a faculty developer, I have worked with outstanding
authentic teachers who were in disciplines that were not in harmony with their nature, as well as many who were. I especially
recall science, mathematics, and some trades teachers (primarily
in welding) who had a marked preference for the feeling function, for working with people. They excelled at helping students
overcome anxiety related to the discipline, build confidence in
their skills and abilities, and appreciate the intrinsic beauty of
the discipline. What these teachers had done was to focus on the
process of teaching and caring for their students, foci which
were well-suited to their natures.

THE INSTITUTION

Hollis (1998, p. 110) writes,

> I once taught at a college whose architecture won a national award. It
> was a series of gray, linear corridors with steel and glass structures and
> interchangeable walls. While it was certainly functional, and created an
> interesting contrast with the surrounding forest, the effect of the build-
> ing itself worked against education. The structure promoted uniformity,
> mobility, interchangeability, and a steady flow of units. These are values
> which best serve an airport, not a college.

It was not just the physical characteristics of the institution that
Hollis found himself at odds with; the building was a metaphor

for the institutional assumptions and values about teaching. The institution we teach in can have a profound impact on how we teach and the degree to which we can feel or be authentic.

Most institutions evolve, over time, so as to ensure a kind of stability. Regardless of the original purpose or the yearly revisions to the mission statement, it becomes the nature of institutions that their functions will continue to be performed in the same manner. An institution is more than the sum of its individuals. Nancy Dixon (1996) points out that institutions acquire patterns of interaction that make it difficult for the system to find out about itself or to develop. Each institution has a culture which may be only partially explicit or conscious; there may be contradictions between an espoused culture and the culture as it exists in practice or as it is perceived by members of the institution.

The institution within which we teach is our most direct and influential context. The institution, of course, includes the smaller groupings of departments and programs that have a clear impact on our practice. Following are just some of the facets of an educational institution's culture that are relevant to how we work:

- the rewards or recognition given for good teaching
- administrative support for professional development
- facilities and resources available
- the physical layout, atmosphere, and comfort of classrooms
- the degree to which colleagues value and talk about teaching
- the social norms of teaching—expectations regarding workload, teaching methods used, amount of interaction with students
- class sizes
- tolerance for failure and drop out rates
- attitudes toward innovations in teaching
- racial, cultural, and gender make-up of student and faculty bodies
- the economic health of the institution
- the existence of partnerships with business or industry
- goals and mission statements

- promotion and tenure procedures
- the presence or absence of a faculty union
- mandatory curricula
- multiple-sectioned courses

The teacher and her students are not an island unto themselves as it may seem from reading many books on teaching. We find ourselves accepting, adapting to, compromising with, challenging, and sometimes rejecting aspects of the institutional culture. I have seen poor teachers go along for the ride for many years in a context that has not ever demanded anything else from them. I have seen excellent teachers leave their profession in frustration at the conflict between themselves and their institution.

In order to be authentic within the institutional context, we first need to be aware of institutional policies, procedures, values, attitudes and norms, both formal and informal. New faculty often feel overwhelmed with the complexity of academic work, including their naivety regarding social networks and unspoken norms (Boice, 1992). Berquist (1994) calls this latter aspect of institutional culture "tacit knowledge." We know, he says, that these values are present and profoundly influence our life, yet they are not directly known to us. It is not only new faculty who are unaware of and uncertain about the context of their institution. Faculty handbooks rarely highlight institutional expectations, and even if they did, these vary from one department or program to another. It is only very recently that researchers and theorists in higher education have started to define just what it is we do (Glassick, Huber, & Maeroff, 1997). In addition, the role of educators is undergoing quite a dramatic transition as colleges and universities deal with financial constraints and shift their focus from the development of individual students to serving business, industry, the community, and the nation. Even those who study education as a discipline have trouble sorting it all out; for those of who teach in our subject area within the context of an institution, it is a greater mystery.

Awareness of our institutional context takes some deliberate effort. We need to join committees where decisions are made, talk to colleagues, talk to administrators, attend "town hall

meetings" and other similar functions, and generally be involved in institutional affairs. No doubt it is hard to find the
time and energy to do this, but the more we understand about
our immediate context, the better we can do our job.

Beyond awareness, the second part of developing authenticity in the context of the institution is taking a stance on issues
being debated and issues we consider important given our values
and beliefs. When a colleague brags that his high failure rate
reflects his high standards, we need to argue against this view,
perhaps bringing up failure rates at a department or program
meeting. When adult students have no access to the library because it closes at 5:00 p.m., we need to approach the library
director to discuss the problem. When an outstanding teacher
is denied tenure because she has not yet published ten articles
in refereed journals, we need to ask that tenure policies be reviewed. Of course, the examples will vary from one institution
to another, and one teacher to another, but my point is that in
order to be true to our own values and beliefs, we need to speak
up when they are violated within our institutional context.

THE COMMUNITY

We belong to more than one community. Geographical
community may be important, if we live and work in an area
where members of a specific locality share government and
have a common cultural heritage. Communities are also social
groups who have common characteristics or interests and perceive themselves as distinct from the larger society on the basis
of their shared qualities. At this level, teachers may see themselves as belonging to a community of educators, or—related to
their discipline—to a community of artists or tradespeople. In
Chapter 6, following a sociological perspective, I define community as a group of people have had a common experience that
has changed or transformed them. Communities may form as
people participate in a retreat, regularly attend a conference,
or survive a traumatic event. Communities may exist within institutions, institutions may be a part of a larger community,

or communities may be entirely independent of institutions. Some institutions—especially small private colleges and universities and community colleges—see themselves as serving communities.

The ways in which the community context influences our teaching, depends, naturally enough, on which type of community we are considering. The geographical community may embrace values or beliefs related to:

• expectations of student employment upon graduation
• the influence of major business or industry interests
• the role of teachers in the community
• the importance of education in general
• the quality or type of education provided
• service provided for minority or ethnic groups

Communities based on shared interests or characteristics may perpetuate values pertaining to:

• educator roles
• the meaning and significance of the discipline
• the purpose of education within a discipline
• assessment and accreditation of people in the field
• the role of the profession or trade in determining educational goals
• the relative importance of theory and practice
• the role of research

Communities that have formed as a result of a significant shared experience may have created values concerning:

• missions, goals, and objectives
• educator roles
• teaching and assessment strategies
• the role of professional or personal development in teaching
• student or faculty rights within the institution

Each of these lists presents examples only. The issues that concern communities vary greatly depending on the type, purpose, and nature of the community. To determine the role of community context in our teaching practice, there are three things to consider.

First, we need to be aware of the communities to which we belong. This may sound simple enough, but there are often social groups with which we are involved that we do not necessarily see as communities at first glance. Geographical communities are generally quite clear, though in some large metropolitan areas, there may be no community as such. Communities based on shared interests can include, in addition to professional groups, groups based on recreational interests, spiritual or religious beliefs, social or cultural interests such as art or music, ethnic origin, and common characteristics such as single parenthood or sexual orientation. Some of these communities may have little relationship to educational values, but often a closer examination reveals that they do. Communities formed as a result of a common experience can emerge from professional experiences such as retreats or conferences, but also from illness, addiction, bereavement, or victimization.

The second part of considering community context involves reviewing the values, beliefs, and assumptions about education inherent in each community of which we are a member. We can pay attention to the values expressed in items about education in local newspaper, radio, and television programs. Involvement in community groups and activities, and just talking about education to others in the community reveals shared social norms. In professional communities, newsletters, conferences, journal articles, and association meetings usually portray commonly-held beliefs about education. Communities that appear to be peripheral to education often exhibit viewpoints on the role of education in those communities. For example, a group of parents fighting against drunk driving may hold the belief that education is the primary tool in their campaign; the assumption is being made that education has a role in social reform.

Third, in order to be authentic educators, we need to participate in discussions of educational beliefs and values within our communities. When we feel strongly about an issue, it is time to speak out. For some teachers, the goal may be to reform the values of their communities; for others, making their own position known and acting on their own beliefs is enough.

STATE AND SOCIETY

The state consists of those public institutions through which the government exercises control. Theoretically, since the institutions are public, power comes from the people, though in modern society, true democratic debate rarely exists. "Public" debates are generally conducted by the media. One of the institutions through which the state exercises control is education. During a dramatic period of change in higher education following the Second World War, universities in the Western world became a public utility (Jones, 1994). As the 1990s drew to a close, we see an even stronger movement toward higher education being controlled by the state in its service to society (Eggins, 1997; Webler, 1997).

By society, I mean the larger community of people who live within a state. Although the word "society" is used in a variety of ways, some of them synonymous with community, in this broader sense of society, people need not have any other connection with each other. In North America, society is pluralistic; that is, it includes an array of social norms and interpretations. However, the *institutions of society* function best when they are unchallenged by individuals. Jarvis (1992, p. 117) raises the question, "if everyone tried to be an authentic person, to learn reflectively and interact in such a way as to encourage the growth and development of other people, would society exist?" Our perspectives or meaning systems are validated through social interaction and supported by institutions of society. Thus we maintain social stability and avoid chaos.

Public institutions, one of which is education, are the machinery used by the state to rule a society. We teach in that context. Within that context, our role is to promote and perpetuate society in order to avoid social chaos. Simultaneously and paradoxically, our role is to challenge the state and to encourage our students to do the same. If our students are to play their part in society, they need to be knowledgeable. Our government needs conforming citizens in order to rule without force, and at the same time, in order to function in a democracy, people need to be reflective and critical in order to represent their interests in the political process.

Most of us practice our teaching craft without a strong awareness of the broader context of state and society. If asked, we might argue that our classes or subject area form but a small corner in the larger picture and are not really relevant to the functioning of society. Yet, every discipline and course contributes to the public institution of higher education, and hence to society. And perhaps less abstractly, we all espouse critical thinking as a goal of higher education.

The authentic teacher needs to have a good awareness of his or her role in education as it exists in relation to the state and society. As Peter Lane pointed out in Chapter 5, authenticity is not a method, it is a "genuine desire to progress, to improve, to grow, and to be more." We must be *mindful* of when we are promoting conformity and when we should dare to dissent. And we should do both so as to act according to our conscious beliefs, values, and assumptions about teaching.

SUMMARY

As Jung (1953–1978) writes in *The Development of Personality*, a part of his twenty-volume collected works:

> Every educator . . . should constantly ask himself whether he is actually fulfilling his teachings in his own person and in his own life, to the best of knowledge and with a clear conscience. Psychotherapy has taught us that in the final reckoning it is not knowledge, not technical skill, that has a curative effect, but the personality of the doctor. And it is the same with education: it presupposes self-education. (par. 240)

In order to fulfill our teachings in our own life, we must maintain a perspective which includes an awareness of our context. If we expect our students not to merely assimilate information from authorities in an unquestioning and uncritical way, we must do the same. Rather than seeing social structures as constraining what we do, we need to look at them closely, consider the meaning systems they portray, ask if and how they support or validate our own values and preferences, and when we experience disjuncture, express our opposition in a justifiable way.

In this chapter, I examined the four levels of context I see as most relevant to teaching practice. The discipline within which we work is composed of one or more kinds of knowledge, perhaps matching our personality preferences but perhaps going against our natural disposition. Institutions develop a culture containing a host of assumptions and values about teaching and learning. We need to know what these are, both the formal policies and procedures and the tacit or unspoken understandings. Within the institution or outside of it, we work in a variety of communities, those based on geography, shared interests, or shared significant experiences. Again, each community has a perspective, articulated or not, on teaching and the role of education within the community. We need to examine those perspectives and determine the degree to which they represent our own views. Finally, both the state and the broader society controlled by the state exert a powerful influence on the way we see teaching and the way we act as teachers. It is likely that we have uncritically assimilated many of the social norms from this larger context. The authentic teacher works toward increasing her awareness of these points of view and tries to separate the paradoxical responsibilities of promoting conformity and fostering critical thinking.

CHAPTER 8

The Transforming Teacher

As we develop, we strengthen our sense of Self in relation to the power of social forces. This process takes place both personally and professionally. Personal development is, at least in part, a process of individuation, of separating the Self from the collective of humanity and learning to express that Self authentically. Similarly, professional development includes identifying who we are as teachers and differentiating that sense of Self from the collective as represented by the discipline, institution, and community within which we practice. Elsewhere, I propose that individuation is a transformative learning process (Cranton, 2000). It is empowering. The empowered teacher becomes free to present herself authentically in the classroom and the community. Thus we can see a kind of circle or spiral of individuation leading to empowerment leading to authenticity and on to further individuation.

Transformative learning occurs when we change a previously unquestioned habit of mind through critical reflection or critical self-reflection (Mezirow, 2000). On a personal level, for example, I may have always accepted that I could not do mathematics, perhaps based on negative experiences in childhood and comments made by a teacher or parent about girls not being good at mathematics. In adulthood, I might find myself in a situation where I realize this habit of mind is not valid. Maybe I can do mathematics. Maybe I was wrong in making that assumption for all these years. I might discuss this with others, try out some activities using mathematics, and reflect on how I came to have this belief in the first place. If I revise my way of thinking, transformative learning takes place. In my teaching, I may have always believed it is my responsibility, as the subject area expert, to give students grades. In all of my prior experience, teachers gave grades. Further, I was of the opinion that grades are the best motivator for learning, and that students cannot assess their own learning. I may then read an article about student self-evaluation, or hear this approach discussed at a conference. I may discover that colleagues use student self-evaluation and talk to them about how and why they do. Through discourse and reflection, I could change my perspective, or my habit of mind, about evaluation of learning.

The transformative learning experience yields a clearer identification of the Self or the Self as Teacher. I can do mathematics; I am separate from the social norm of my childhood in which girls could do not do mathematics. I do not necessarily need to be the one to evaluate student learning; I am separate from the community of educators who believes that teachers are responsible for grading.

In this chapter, I first discuss personal growth as an outcome of transformative learning, in relation to our sense of Self, our psychological type preferences, our experiences, and our values. I then examine transformative experiences leading to professional growth, especially in relation to the social norms of the Good Teacher and the identification of the *teacher within* and the *teacher without*. In the third part of the chapter, I argue that personal growth feeds into professional development. Finally, I propose that our professional development, in turn, helps us to continue to transform and individuate in our personal lives.

PERSONAL GROWTH

Personal growth through transformative learning is an empowering process. We become free from the constraint of unquestioned or distorted assumptions and beliefs about who we are. Growth takes place in at least three ways: as a product of the normal transitions through stages of adult development, as a result of traumatic or peak experiences in life, and as an outcome of deliberate, conscious efforts to change. In Chapters 1 and 2, I suggested exercises in which we could contemplate our basic sense of Self, our psychological preferences, the experiences that have shaped us, and our most cherished values. In each of these exercises, I suggested reflection on two questions—how we came to have the self-perception, and why the self-perception is important. These questions, particularly the latter one, which addresses the premise of our assumptions about ourselves, constitute critical self-reflection, the basis for transformative learning. We may ask ourselves such questions as we grow older in the natural course of events, or as a result of a dramatic change in our lives, such as a change in career or the loss of a mate, or as a part of a purposeful effort to engage in personal development.

When we make conscious and mindful changes in our sense of Self, psychological preferences, or values, and when we understand experiences in new ways, we take another step in the lifelong journey of individuation. That is, we identify our Self, an individual, as separate from those people who have shaped us over the years and those with whom we now live and work. Becoming an authentic teacher is predicated on a continued deepening sense of who we are.

Short of sitting back and waiting for the next life stage or engineering traumatic events, how can we facilitate our own personal growth through transformative learning? I give some suggestions here; in my book, *Personal Empowerment through Type*, I provide considerably more detail (Cranton, 1998c).

Transformative learning is stimulated by encountering viewpoints that are discrepant with our own. If we only read things that support our views and avoid experiences that might lead to questioning our beliefs, it is unlikely we will engage in critical self-reflection. In today's world, it is fairly easy to encounter alternative points of view. Through the Internet, media, travel, and reading, we can expose ourselves to different values and beliefs. We can deliberately participate in conversations and events where we know the values expressed will be at odds with our own. This does not mean we need to adopt them; the goal is increased awareness of alternatives, some of which may lead to questioning of our assumptions. The trick is to make ourselves genuinely open to new options and choices.

Transformative growth is also based on discourse with others. By discourse (as opposed to conversation or discussion), Mezirow (1991) means a specialized kind of dialogue devoted to justifying an interpretation or belief. Rather than trying to convince others of our own point of view through charisma or winning arguments, discourse involves weighing supporting evidence, assessing reasons, and examining alternative perspectives. The goals are to understand different ways of thinking, search for common ground, and resolve differences. Joining or initiating discussion groups, engaging in correspondence with others on issues of mutual interest, and genuinely seeking to understand others through listening and questioning can foster good discourse.

Transformative learning involves examining assumptions and beliefs that have been uncritically assimilated. Many such assumptions are not articulated or conscious, we simply act on them because we have always done so. If I grew up in a family and community that valued the acquisition of money and possessions for their own sake, I may go on well into adulthood acquiring more money and possessions than I need without much thought as to why I am doing this. Or, I may be unhappy and frustrated at not being able to acquire money, without understanding why this bothers me. It is hard to access unarticulated assumptions. Exposing ourselves to alternative viewpoints helps, as does engaging in discourse, but often this is not enough. Our blind spots have deep roots. Examining critical incidents in our lives, especially through conversation with another person whom we trust may reveal assumptions. Other potentially useful exercises include reversing roles with another person who has a different perspective and expressing ourselves from that person's point of view, taking our values and arguing for the opposite value, and writing letters to ourselves at earlier or later stages of life. Any activity which forces us to look at what we believe, how we came to believe it, why we still believe it, and what the consequences are of continuing to believe it or choosing not to believe it has the potential to foster the critical self-reflection necessary for transformative learning.

PROFESSIONAL GROWTH

Unfortunately, professional development for teachers is often viewed as the acquisition of new techniques or skills. Our search for growth may focus on finding the "right way" of doing things. If only, we think, we can hit on the right approach, our students will be eager, motivated, and excel in their learning. It does not work like this. Knowledge about teaching is primarily communicative in nature rather than instrumental (see Chapter 7, my discussion of the context of discipline, for an elaboration on kinds of knowledge). Knowledge about teaching is based on an interest in understanding and communicating with others. There are few objective and absolute truths; cause and effect principles are rare. Professional growth is not mainly about learning to prepare colored overhead transparencies or bringing the Internet into the classroom. It is about questioning how we relate to students, challenging the social norms surrounding teaching, critically reflecting on our work, and learning who we are as authentic teachers.

Our habits of mind regarding teaching may fall into several different categories.

- Sociolinguistic habits of mind are those which are based on social norms, customs, and socialization. The Good Teacher (Chapter 3) is essentially this. Although it is derived in part from research, our concept of a good teacher has become a social norm, one which none of us can live up to.
- Epistemic habits of mind are those based on knowledge and how we acquire knowledge. What we have learned about teaching skills, techniques, and roles through reading or attending conferences may become epistemic habits of mind. Our concept of the *teacher without* (Chapter 4) may be based

on epistemic habits of mind about teaching. The way we
acquire knowledge about teaching—through experience,
theoretical reading, working with others, imagining alternatives—is also a part of our epistemic habit of mind.

- Psychological habits of mind are those related to our self-concept, personality traits, confidence, and, generally, the way we
  see ourselves. Our *teacher within* (Chapter 4) may form a psychological habit of mind.
- Moral or ethical habits of mind have to do with moral norms,
  professionalism, conscience, and our view of ethical practice.
- Philosophical habits of mind are those which incorporate our
  broader view of education in society. Many of the issues discussed in Chapter 7 may represent philosophical habits of
  mind.

The transforming teacher works to articulate her habits of
mind, question them, reflect on them, engage in discourse, and
be open to alternatives. When we are acquiring or revising instrumental knowledge, we empirically test ideas or concepts to
determine their truth. Knowledge about teaching, however, is
primarily communicative in nature, and we justify our beliefs
through rational discourse, with a goal to coming to a best judgment—a judgment which may be later altered as new evidence,
arguments, or viewpoints become available.

There is a considerable emphasis on rational thought in
transformative learning theory, and it has been criticized on that
basis (for example, see Dirkx, 1997). Following the rational approach to transformation, we could be led to the conclusion that
individuals who are more perceptive (intuitive or sensing) in nature (see Chapter 1) would be less likely to transform and this
does not sit right. I have struggled with this issue in several of
my books (for example, Cranton, 1994) and most recently have
come to think that the *judgments* involved in transformative
learning must, indeed, be made with either the thinking or feeling function, but this does not imply that a perceptive person
does not do this. Those of us who have a psychological preference for a perceptive function may see the process differently,

experience it differently, but in the end, if it is a mindful transformation, we would use our auxiliary judgmental function in revising a frame of reference (see Cranton, 2000, for a more detailed discussion).

How can we work toward transformative professional development? Most of the exercises and suggestions throughout this book are designed so as to encourage an increased awareness of habits of mind related to teaching. Writing an educational autobiography, reviewing values and significant experiences, understanding psychological type preferences, analyzing and reflecting on teaching strengths, reviewing others' stories, contemplating relations with students, and reflecting on the context of teaching all foster a deeper understanding of our frames of reference or habits of mind related to teaching. To stimulate critical reflection and critical self-reflection on these habits of mind, I give some further recommendations here.

- Question assumptions about teaching by asking, "Was there a time when I did not hold this belief?" "Was there an influential person in my life who held this belief?" "Is this a commonly held belief in the institution, community, or larger society?" "If I did not believe this, how would I act differently?"
- Imagine alternative points of view through brainstorming with colleagues or students, visualization exercises, or writing or speaking from a point of view other than your own.
- Initiate a "Let's Talk about Teaching" group at your institution, engaging the help of a faculty developer if one is available. Suggest diverse and unusual topics.
- Do "action research" in your classroom. Collect information from students as to their perspectives on teaching; try out an innovation and collect student feedback; implement unusual suggestions from students.
- Keep a teaching journal in which you not only record what happens and how things are going, but also question and speculate on your practice.
- Write book reviews, articles, or newsletter items criticizing current perspectives on teaching and learning.

- Take on the job of providing a critique of the curriculum in your program or department. Ask serious questions about why things are done the way they are done.

Activities such as these help to encourage critical reflection and self-reflection on teaching. Once we start asking questions and considering alternative viewpoints, it becomes almost impossible to stop. Often, we will decide to maintain our current perspective, but it will be better justified in our minds. Sometimes, critical reflection leads to a gradual shift in thinking— incremental transformation. And, perhaps less often, we suddenly see things in a completely different way, like looking at a figure-ground drawing in which there are two pictures embedded and finally seeing the second picture. This is an epochal transformative learning experience. It may be awkward, confusing, or even painful to give up an old habit of mind; Scott (1997) speaks of the grieving that takes place when we transform a perspective. If transformative learning is individuation—separation from the uncritically assimilated beliefs of the collective— we are detaching ourselves, and this feels lonely for a time. But, in the end, it is continual learning and growth which keeps us alive, genuine, and authentic in our teaching practice. We may find other like-minded souls and regroup, form a new community, or find new and more authentic ways of relating to our previous community without giving up our insights.

DEVELOPING SELF AS TEACHER

For the authentic teacher, personal growth and development leads to changes in teaching. In my own experience, an important example comes to mind. About ten years ago, a colleague introduced me to Jung's ([1921] 1971) model of psychological type. Until that time, I had worked hard at being more outgoing than I was by nature. I forced myself to attend parties, travel, have guests for dinner—all things I did not, but thought I should, enjoy. I was also often appalled at others' perceptions of me as uncaring. Through reading Jung's work, I came to see that my preferences for introversion over extraversion and thinking over feeling were a part of a pattern of human differences that Jung had observed. Although there are fewer people, especially in North American society, who prefer introversion over extraversion, and although women are stereotyped as being more caring than men, I saw my psychological type profile as a valid way of being for the first time. This had a significant impact on my personal life; I became more comfortable with who I was and stopped, for the most part, putting myself into anxiety-provoking situations. Over time, I was then able to learn to enjoy social gatherings and travel in a way that suited my nature, and I developed what was for me an authentic way of expressing caring.

This personal journey had an important effect on my teaching. Rather than thinking I should be a dynamic and charismatic lecturer, a person who could tell funny and relevant stories, and mesmerize students with my enthusiasm, I let myself be calm and quiet in the classroom. I learned to facilitate others' discussions, an approach that also happened to suit my subject area much more than what I had been trying to do. I gave myself time to think something through, and sometimes my silence allowed students to reflect as well, but other times, it encouraged them to speak for themselves on the topic. There was not a dramatic change in my teaching from one day to the next, but rather a gradual emerging of my sense of Self as I worked with one class after another over the next years. At the personal level, the transformation in my psychological habit of mind was quite dramatic, but perhaps not epochal. In my teaching practice, the transformation was incremental as I slowly tried one small change after another, each building on the previous one, and each step leading me to be more congruent with who I was outside of the classroom.

In Exercise 8.1, I suggest a process for contemplating how personal development has or can contribute to professional growth. The first step is to recall a period of personal transformation and growth. I then recommend we reflect on how this personal change influenced teaching. Sometimes we keep our personal and professional lives separate in ways that do not al-

Exercise 8.1 Personal Growth and Teaching

Part One. Consider a time in your life when you experienced a transformation or change in your personal life. Take a few notes on the situation. What kind of habit of mind was revised? How did it come about? Who was involved?

_____

_____

_____

_____

Part Two. List any ways in which your personal change influenced your teaching, whether they be small or large changes. Consider how you felt about teaching in general as well as your teaching methods, relations with students, approaches to planning, and evaluation strategies.

_____

_____

_____

Part Three. Now consider other ways in which your personal transformation could have affected your teaching, but did not. For each, ask yourself why the change did not filter into your teaching practice.

_____

_____

_____

low one to influence the other. In the third part of the exercise, I advise considering other ways in which the change could have affected teaching but did not, and why this was the case.

The very process of bringing together personal change and teaching in our minds and thinking about how one contributes to the other can sometimes lead to new insights. It may be worthwhile to repeat this exercise with various personal transformations.

DEVELOPING TEACHER AS SELF

Transformations in our teaching habits of mind can also, in turn, alter our personal lives. One good example that I have experienced to some extent myself and have seen several colleagues and friends go through has to do with power and control in teaching. Many of us believe a good teacher has control over his class, a responsibility to keep things on track. We see the position of educator as one of power, authority, and responsibility. If our students do not learn what we expect them to learn, we have done something wrong. If someone does not contribute to a discussion or pays little attention to what we say, it is up to us to do something about it. This habit of mind has obvious roots in the traditional education many of us experienced—students sitting quietly in rows while the teacher talked, with a sharp punishment to follow if anyone spoke out of line.

As we read the literature that encourages us to be co-learners, to use interactive methods, to encourage a noisy and fun-filled classroom, some of us have changed our assumptions about teacher control and power. We have discovered the good things that happen when students talk to each other, move around, make choices, and assume responsibility for their own learning. The transformation may be difficult and uncomfortable. We may be challenged by students, colleagues, or administrators. We may be moving away from the social norms of our institution or community. We may doubt ourselves and wonder if we are doing our job, but after awhile, giving up position power in the classroom feels right to us.

What can happen next is equally exciting. The growth we experience as teachers can filter into our personal lives in a variety of ways. Perhaps we change the way we relate to our children or other family members; perhaps we stop feeling frustrated and angry when we cannot control the fools who continually mess up our telephone bill or misplace our dry cleaning. Learning to let go in teaching allows us to see the joy in letting go, and it is only natural to want to carry that into other spheres of our lives.

This is but one example. In Exercise 8.2, I propose we generate other examples of how teaching transformations have changed our personal life.

When we learn to listen to our students and to ask the kind of question that leads to reflection, these need not be skills that stay in the classroom. When we revise a broader habit of mind related to teaching, we have changed our Self—being a teacher is a part of our Self. The change leaves ripples in the way we walk in the rest of the world. When Self and Teacher are integrated, as they are for the authentic teacher, the transforming teacher is a part of the transforming Self. As individuals, we differentiate ourselves from the collective of humanity; as teachers we separate ourselves from the community of educators.

SUMMARY

Teaching from the heart means teaching from the depths of who we are with the hope that we will touch the hearts of those with whom we work. To begin discovering the core of who we are requires that we work to become aware of our beliefs and values. (Apps, 1996, p. 64)

As we work to become aware of our beliefs and values, we articulate them, discuss them with others, reflect on them, and sometimes transform them. Through a continual process of reflection and transformation, we find our own identity, as individuals in our personal life and as teachers in our professional life. We no longer go with what others do and say without thought because we have learned who we are and how to think for ourselves. To be an authentic teacher is to be a transform-

---

Exercise 8.2 Professional Growth and Personal Change

Part One. Recall a time when you changed a teaching perspective, either gradually or as a result of a dramatic incident. What assumptions, beliefs, or values changed? Who was involved? Why did this change take place?

_____

_____

_____

Part Two. Consider ways in which the teaching transformation influenced your life outside the classroom. How did you act differently in the classroom? Were there parallel changes in your personal life?

_____

_____

_____

---

ing teacher, for we cannot be authentic without awareness of our beliefs and values, and we cannot be aware without contemplating how we came to have these values and how well they serve us.

Authentic teachers are true to themselves in the classroom. Their personal and professional beings are integrated. They may consciously decide to do or not to do things in the classroom that they would do in their home, but this is not because they are separate people, or one person playing a role, but because they have deliberately worked to understand what it means to them, as individuals, to be teachers.

Increased self-awareness and separation of the Self from the group through individuation empowers us to express ourselves authentically in our work and in the community of educators. Authentic expression leads to further self-understanding as we encounter people and situations at odds with our Self. The transforming teacher experiences a spiral of individuation, empowerment, and authenticity, a lifelong journey of growth and development.

In this chapter, I looked at how transformative learning takes place in both our personal and professional lives. Transformative learning results from examining habits of mind that we had absorbed from our community and culture without being aware of having done so. When we take these habits and look at them closely, discuss them with others, and discard or revise those we find limiting or invalid, we are working toward drawing a clearer picture of ourselves.

When we grow toward a clearer perception of ourselves as individuals in our personal life, this will influence our teaching selves if Teacher and Self are integrated. Similarly, when we develop as teachers, our changed perspectives filter into our personal lives. The authentic transforming teacher is engaged in a lifelong journey of individuation. Since there is no artificial separation between the person and the teacher, all growth is relevant to both personal and professional life.

REFERENCES

Anderson, J. R. (1983). *The architecture of cognition.* Cambridge, MA: Harvard University Press.

Apps, J. (1996). *Teaching from the heart.* Malabar, FL: Krieger.

Bassett, D. S., & Jackson, L. (1994). Applying the model to a variety of adult learning situations. In L. Jackson, & R. S. Caffarella (Eds.), *Experiential learning: A new approach* (pp. 55–62). New Directions for Adult and Continuing Education, no. 62. San Francisco: Jossey-Bass.

Beckman, M. (1990). Collaborative learning: Preparation for the workplace and democracy. *College Teaching, 38*(4), 128–133.

Berquist, W. (1994). Unconscious values with four academic cultures. In E. C. Wadsworth (Ed.), *To improve the academy* (pp. 349–372). Valdosta, GA: The Professional and Organizational Development Network in Higher Education.

Boice, R. (1992). *The new faculty member.* San Francisco: Jossey-Bass.

Brailey, J. (1998). The conversion of a skeptic. In P. Cranton (Ed.), *Psychological Type in Action* (pp. 42–49). Sneedville, TN: Psychological Type Press.

Brookfield, S. (1990). *The skillful teacher.* San Francisco: Jossey-Bass.

Brookfield, S. (1991). *Developing critical thinkers.* San Francisco: Jossey-Bass.

Brookfield, S. (1995). *Becoming a critically reflective teacher.* San Francisco: Jossey-Bass.

Brookfield, S., & Preskill, S. (1999). *Discussion as a way of teaching: Tools and techniques for democratic classrooms.* San Francisco: Jossey-Bass.

Bruner, J. (1986). *Actual minds, possible words.* Cambridge, MA: Harvard University Press.

Carbone, E. (1999). Students behaving badly in large classes. In S. M. Richardson (Ed.), *Promoting civility: A teaching challenge* (pp. 35–

44). New Directions for Teaching and Learning, no. 77. San Francisco: Jossey-Bass.

Chickering, A. W., & Gamson, Z. E. (Eds.). (1991). *Applying the seven principles for good practice in undergraduate education.* New Directions for Teaching and Learning, no. 47. San Francisco: Jossey-Bass.

Clark, J. E. (1997). Of writing, imagination, and dialogue: A transformative experience. In P. Cranton (Ed.), *Transformative learning in action: Insights from practice* (pp. 13–22). New Directions for Adult and Continuing Education, no. 74. San Francisco: Jossey-Bass.

Cohen, N. H. (1995). *Mentoring adult learners: A guide for educators and trainers.* Malabar, FL: Krieger.

Connelly, F. M., & Clandinin, D. J. (1994). Telling teaching stories. *Teacher Education Quarterly, 21*(1), 145–158.

Cranton, P. (1994). *Understanding and promoting transformative learning.* San Francisco: Jossey-Bass.

Cranton, P. (1996). Types of groups. In S. Imel (Ed.), *Learning in groups: Exploring fundamental principles, new uses, and emerging opportunities* (pp. 25–32). New Directions for Adult and Continuing Education, no. 71. San Francisco: Jossey-Bass.

Cranton, P. (1998a). *Fostering transformative learning.* Paper presented at the First Annual Conference on Transformative Learning, New York.

Cranton, P. (1998b). *No one way: Teaching and learning in higher education.* Toronto: Wall and Emerson.

Cranton, P. (1998c). *Personal empowerment through type.* Sneedville, TN: Psychological Type Press.

Cranton, P. (2000). Fostering transformative learning: Considering individual differences among people. In J. Mezirow (Ed.), *The transformative power of learning.* San Francisco: Jossey-Bass.

Cranton, P., & Knoop, R. (1994). *The PET Type Check.* Sneedville, TN: Psychological Type Press.

Cranton, P., & Knoop, R. (1995). Assessing psychological type: The PET Type Check. *General, Social, and Genetic Psychological Monographs, 121*(2), 247–274.

Cuban, L. (1993). *How teachers taught: Constancy and change in American classrooms 1890–1990.* New York: Teachers College Press.

Curran, C. A. (1978). *Understanding: An essential ingredient in human belonging.* East Dubuque, IL: Counseling-Learning Publications.

Daloz, L. A. (1986). *Effective teaching and mentoring: Realizing the transformational power of adult learning experiences.* San Francisco: Jossey-Bass.

Davis, B. G. (1993). *Tools for teaching.* San Francisco: Jossey-Bass.

De Bono, E. (1970). *Lateral thinking: Creativity step by step.* New York: Harper and Row.

Dewey, J. (1916). *Democracy and education.* New York: Macmillan.

Dewey, J. (1933). *How we think.* New York: Heath.

Dewey, J. (1938). *Experience and education.* New York: Collier Books.

Dirkx, J. (1997). Nurturing soul in adult learning. In P. Cranton (Ed.), *Transformative learning in action: Insights from practice* (pp. 79–88). New Directions for Adult and Continuing Education, no. 74. San Francisco: Jossey-Bass.

Dixon, N. M. (1996). *Perspectives on dialogue: Making talk developmental for individuals and organizations.* Greensboro, NC: Center for Creative Leadership.

Eggins, H. (1997). The impact of government policy on university faculty. In P. Cranton (Ed.), *Universal challenges in faculty work: Fresh perspectives from around the world,* (pp. 23–30). New Directions for Teaching and Learning, no. 72. San Francisco: Jossey-Bass.

Ewert, G. D. (1991). Habermas and education: A comprehensive overview of the influence of Habermas in educational literature. *Review of Educational Research, 61*(3), 345–378.

Fiechtner, S. B., & Davis, E. A. (1992). Why some groups fail: A survey of students' experiences with learning groups. In A. Goodsell, M. Maher, V. Tinto, and Associates, *Collaborative learning: A sourcebook for higher education* (pp. 59–67). University Park: National Center on Postsecondary Teaching, Learning and Assessment, Pennsylvania State University.

Gardner, H. (1993). *Frames of Mind: The Theory of Multiple Intelligences (10th Anniversary Edition).* New York: Basic Books.

Glassick, C. E., Huber, M. T., & Maeroff, G. I. (1997). *Scholarship assessed: Evaluation of the professoriate.* San Francisco: Jossey-Bass.

Guilford, J. P. (1950). Creativity. *American Psychologist, 5,* 444–454.

Guilford, J. P. (1959). Three faces of intellect, *American Psychologist, 14,* 469–479.

Habermas, J. (1971). *Knowledge and human interests.* Boston: Beacon Press.

Hauenstein, A.D. (1998). *A conceptual framework for educational objectives: A holistic approach to traditional taxonomies.* Lanham, MD: University Press of America.

Heimlich, J. E., & Norland, E. (1994). *Developing teaching style in adult education.* San Francisco: Jossey-Bass.

Heimstra, R., & Brockett, R. G. (1998). From mentor to partner: Lessons from a personal journey. In I. M. Saltiel, A. Sgroi, & R. G. Brockett (Eds.), *The power and potential of collaborative learning partnerships* (pp. 43–52). New Directions for Adult and Continuing Education, no. 79. San Francisco: Jossey-Bass.

Henry, E., Huntley, J., McKamey, C., & Harper, L. T. (1995). *To be a teacher: Voices from the classroom.* Thousand Oaks, CA: Corwin Press.

Hilgard, E. R., & Bower, G. H. (1966). *Theories of learning.* New York: Appleton-Century-Crofts.

Hollis, J. (1998). *The Eden project: In Search of the magical other.* Toronto: Inner City Books.

Hudson, L. (1968). *Frames of mind: Ability, percpetion, and self-perception in the arts and sciences.* London: Methuen.

Jarvis, P. (1992). *Paradoxes of learning: On becoming an individual in society.* San Francisco: Jossey-Bass.

Jones, G. (1994). The political analysis of higher education: An introduction to the symposium on the university and democracy. *Interchange, 25*(1), 1–10.

Jung, C. (1971). *Psychological types.* Princeton, NJ: Princeton University Press. (Originally published in 1921.)

Jung, C. (1953–1978). *The collected works* (Bollingen Series XX). 20 vols. Princeton, NJ: Princeton University Press.

Kincheloe, J. L. (1991). *Teachers as researchers: Qualitative inquiry as a path to empowerment.* London: Falmer Press.

King, P. M., & Kitchener, K. S. (1994). *Developing reflective judgment.* San Francisco: Jossey-Bass.

Kingwell, M. (1995). *A civil tongue.* University Park: Pennsylvania State University Press.

Kohl, H. (1994). *I won't learn from you: And other thoughts on creative maladjustment.* New York: New Press.

Kolb, D. A. (1984). *Experiential learning.* Englewood Cliffs, NJ: Prentice Hall.

Kuhlenschmidt, S. L. (1999). Promoting internal civility: Understanding our beliefs about teaching and students. In S. M. Richardson (Ed.), *Promoting civility: A teaching challenge* (pp. 45–58). New Directions for Teaching and Learning, no. 77. San Francisco: Jossey-Bass.

Lewis, L. H., & Williams, C. J. (1994). Experiential learning: Past and present. In L. Jackson & R. S. Caffarella (Eds.), *Experiential learning: A new approach* (pp. 5–16). New Directions for Adult and Continuing Education, no. 62. San Francisco: Jossey-Bass.

Lieberman, A., & Miller, L. (1991). Revisiting the social realities of teaching. In A. Lieberman & L. Miller (Eds.), *Staff development for educators in the 1990's: New demands, new realities, new perspectives.* New York: Teachers College Press.

MacKeracher, D. (1996). *Making sense of adult learning.* Toronto: Culture Concepts.

Maslow, A. H. (1968). *Toward a psychology of being.* New York: Van Nostrand.

Merriam, S. B., & Brockett, R. G. (1997). *The profession and practice of adult education: An introduction.* San Francisco: Jossey-Bass.

Mezirow, J. (2000). Learning to think like an adult: Transformation theory—An update. In J. Mezirow (Ed.), *The transformative power of learning.* San Francisco: Jossey-Bass.

Mezirow, J. (1991). *Transformative dimensions of adult learning.* San Francisco: Jossey-Bass.

Miller, A. (1991). *Personality types: A modern synthesis.* Calgary: University of Calgary Press.

Myers, I. (1995). *Gifts differing.* Palo Alto, CA: Consulting Psychologists Press.

Nesbit, T. (1998). Teaching in adult education: Opening the black box. *Adult Education Quarterly, 48*(3), 157–170.

Rogers, C. (1951). *Client-centered therapy.* Boston: Houghton Mifflin.

Rogers, C. (1969). *Freedom to learn.* Columbus: Charles E. Merrill.

Scott, S. (1997). The grieving soul in the transformative process. In P. Cranton (Ed.), *Transformative learning in action: Insights from practice* (pp. 41–50). New Directions for Adult and Continuing Education, no. 74. San Francisco: Jossey-Bass.

Sgroi, A., & Saltiel, I. M. (1998). Human connections. In I. M. Saltiel, A. Sgroi, & R. Brockett (Eds.), *The power and potential of collaborative learning partnerships,* (pp. 87–92). New Directions for Adult and Continuing Education, no. 79. San Francisco: Jossey-Bass.

Sharp, D. (1987). *Personality types: Jung's model of typology.* Toronto: Inner City Books.

Sharp, D. (1995). *Who am I, really?* Toronto: Inner City Books.

Skinner, B. F. (1953). *Science and human behavior.* New York: Crowell-Collier and Macmillan.

Tennant, M., & Pogson, P. (1995). *Learning and change in the adult years: A developmental perspective.* San Francisco: Jossey-Bass.

Torrance, E. P. (1962). *Guiding creative talent.* Englewood Cliffs, NJ: Prentice Hall.

Torrance, E. P. (1963). *Education and the creative potential.* Minneapolis: University of Minnesota Press.

van Halen-Faber, C. (1997). Encouraging critical reflection in preservice teacher education: A narrative of a personal learning journey. In P. Cranton (Ed.), *Transformative learning in action: Insights from practice* (pp. 51–60). New Directions for Adult and Continuing Education, no. 74. San Francisco: Jossey-Bass.

Vesey, G., & Foulkes, P. (1990). *Collins dictionary of philosophy.* London: Collins.

Webler, W-D. (1997). Goals of higher education curricula. In P. Cranton (Ed.), *Universal challenges in faculty work: Fresh perspectives from around the world* (pp. 81–90). New Directions for Teaching and Learning, no. 72. San Francisco: Jossey-Bass.

INDEX